THIS WORKBOOK BELONGS TO:

_____

STUDENT WORKBOOK
OF MICE AND MEN

Use this workbook to get the most out of your reading.
Answer questions completely and thoughtfully.

COPYRIGHT INFORMATION

This is copyrighted material.

The purchaser may copy the student materials
for his or her classroom use only.
It may not be copied or distributed for any other purpose
without written permission from the publisher.

No portion may be posted on the Internet
without written permission from the publisher.

Copyright violations are prosecuted to the fullest extent of the law
and are subject to a minimum of a $500.00 fine,
imposed by the publisher
in addition to any other legal judgments obtained.

ISBN 978-1-60249-505-0
Copyright 2014
All Rights Reserved

Table Of Contents

Chapter 1
    Reading Activity 1: True or False 7
    Reading Activity 2: Analyzing Passages 10
    Reading Activity 3: Characters, Lexicon, & Diction 13
    Reading Activity 4: Action, Character, Decision 15
    Reading Activity 5: Figurative Language 16
    Reading Activity 6: Elements of Fiction & Literary Devices 17
    Reading Activity 7: Meaning And Inferences 20
    Writing Activity 1: What Is Friendship 23
    Suggested Writing Assignments 26
    Quick-Write Assignments 27

Chapter 2
    Reading Activity 1: True or False 31
    Reading Activity 2: Analyzing Passages 34
    Reading Activity 3: Physical Attributes & Characterization 37
    Reading Activity 4: Action, Character, Decision 38
    Reading Activity 5: Figurative Language 39
    Reading Activity 6: Elements of Fiction & Literary Devices 40
    Reading Activity 7: Meaning And Inferences 42
    Writing Activity 1: What Is Masculinity? 45
    Suggested Writing Assignments 49
    Quick-Write Assignments 50

Chapter 3
    Reading Activity 1: True or False 53
    Reading Activity 2: Analyzing Passages 56
    Reading Activity 3: Foil Character Study 58
    Reading Activity 4: Action, Character, Decision 59
    Reading Activity 5: Figurative Language 60
    Reading Activity 6: Elements of Fiction & Literary Devices 61
    Reading Activity 7: Meaning And Inferences 63
    Writing Activity 1: How Is Weakness Or Strength Determined? 67
    Suggested Writing Assignments 71
    Quick-Write Assignments 72

Chapter 4
    Reading Activity 1: True or False 75
    Reading Activity 2: Analyzing Passages 78
    Reading Activity 3: Direct vs. Indirect Characterization 81
    Reading Activity 4: Action, Character, Decision 82
    Reading Activity 5: Figurative Language 83
    Reading Activity 6: Elements of Fiction & Literary Devices 84
    Reading Activity 7: Meaning And Inferences 86
    Writing Activity 1: What Are The Effects Of Isolation? 89
    Suggested Writing Assignments 92
    Quick-Write Assignments 93

Table Of Contents, Continued

Chapter 5
    Reading Activity 1: True or False 97
    Reading Activity 2: Analyzing Passages 100
    Reading Activity 3: Round Characters or Stereotypes? 103
    Reading Activity 4: Action, Character, Decision 104
    Reading Activity 5: Figurative Language 105
    Reading Activity 6: Elements of Fiction & Literary Devices 106
    Reading Activity 7: Meaning And Inferences 108
    Writing Activity 1: What Does Curley's Wife Symbolize? 110
    Suggested Writing Assignments 113
    Quick-Write Assignments 114

Chapter 6
    Reading Activity 1: True or False 117
    Reading Activity 2: Analyzing Passages 120
    Reading Activity 3: A Closer Look At Lennie 123
    Reading Activity 4: Action, Character, Decision 124
    Reading Activity 5: Figurative Language 125
    Reading Activity 6: Elements of Fiction & Literary Devices 126
    Reading Activity 7: Meaning And Inferences 128
    Writing Activity 1: Is Murder An Act of Friendship? 131
    Suggested Writing Assignments 134
    Quick-Write Assignments 135

Overview
    Reading Activity 1: True or False 139
    Reading Activity 2: Analyzing Passages 142
    Reading Activity 3: Characters, Motivation, & Dreams 144
    Reading Activity 4: Action, Character, Decision 146
    Reading Activity 5: Figurative Language 147
    Reading Activity 6: Elements of Fiction & Literary Devices 148
    Reading Activity 7: Meaning And Inferences 149
    Writing Activity 1: Sharing A Common Dream 152
    Suggested Writing Assignments 155
    Quick-Write Assignments 156

MATERIALS: CHAPTER 1
OF MICE AND MEN

Reading Activity 1: True or False?

Reading Activity 2: Analyzing Passages

Reading Activity 3: Characters, Lexicon, and Diction

Reading Activity 4: Action, Character, Decision

Reading Activity 5: Figurative Language

Reading Activity 6: Elements of Fiction & Literary Devices

Reading Activity 7: Meaning and Inferences

Writing Activity 1: What Is Friendship?

Suggested Writing Assignments

Quick-Write Assignments

NOTES
OF MICE AND MEN

Of Mice And Men Chapter 1: True or False?

Write *True* or *False* in the blank next to each statement. Below the statement, explain why you chose true or false, referencing the text to support your choices.

_____ 1. Lennie is not capable of traveling by himself.

_____ 2. Lennie lies, but he does not do it maliciously.

_____ 3. Lennie was believed to have attacked a woman in Weed.

Of Mice And Men Chapter 1 True or False? Page 2

_____ 4. Lennie believes that his dream is attainable.

_____ 5. George believes that Lennie's behavior will not cause another crisis.

_____ 6. George is more impatient with Lennie than he is patient and understanding.

Of Mice And Men Chapter 1 True or False? Evaluation

List Your Group's Members: Your Group's Question # _____

_____   _____   _____

_____   _____   _____

1 = No, Not At All **2** = A Little **3** = Some **4** = Yes **5** = Yes, Very Well

Evaluation of Question # ___
Does the explanation support the answer of true or false?   1 2 3 4 5
Is there good textual evidence to support the answer?   1 2 3 4 5
Is the answer clearly stated?   1 2 3 4 5
                        Total Score _____ of a possible 15 points

Evaluation of Question # ___
Does the explanation support the answer of true or false?   1 2 3 4 5
Is there good textual evidence to support the answer?   1 2 3 4 5
Is the answer clearly stated?   1 2 3 4 5
                        Total Score _____ of a possible 15 points

Evaluation of Question # ___
Does the explanation support the answer of true or false?   1 2 3 4 5
Is there good textual evidence to support the answer?   1 2 3 4 5
Is the answer clearly stated?   1 2 3 4 5
                        Total Score _____ of a possible 15 points

Evaluation of Question # ___
Does the explanation support the answer of true or false?   1 2 3 4 5
Is there good textual evidence to support the answer?   1 2 3 4 5
Is the answer clearly stated?   1 2 3 4 5
                        Total Score _____ of a possible 15 points

Evaluation of Question # ___
Does the explanation support the answer of true or false?   1 2 3 4 5
Is there good textual evidence to support the answer?   1 2 3 4 5
Is the answer clearly stated?   1 2 3 4 5
                        Total Score _____ of a possible 15 points

Of Mice And Men Chapter 1 Analyzing Passages

Answer the questions following the quotations completely.

1. "…[Lennie] walked heavily, dragging his feet a little, way a bear drags his paws. His arms did not swing at his sides, but hung loosely….Lennie dabbled his big paw in the water and wiggled his fingers so the water arose in little splashes; rings widened across the pool on the other side and came back again."

How is Lennie described physically? Why is it significant?

2. "What you want of a dead mouse, anyways?"
"I could pet it with my thumb while we walked along," said Lennie.

Why does Lennie want the mouse? How does he benefit from having it? What does this reveal about his judgment?

3. "[Lennie] said gently, "George… I ain't got mine. I musta lost it." He looked down at the ground in despair.

"You never had none, you crazy bastard. I got both of 'em here. Think I'd let you carry your own work card?"

Lennie grinned with relief.

How does this interchange characterize their relationship? How does "crazy bastard" contrast with George's care for Lennie?

Of Mice And Men Chapter 1 Analyzing Passages Page 2

4. "That ranch we're goin' to is right down there about a quarter mile. We're gonna go in an' see the boss. Now, look—I'll give him the work tickets, but you ain't gonna say a word. You jus' stand there and don't say nothing. If he finds out what a crazy bastard you are, we won't get no job, but if he sees ya work before he hears ya talk, we're set."

What does this suggest about Lennie's ability to work? How does that contrast with his ability to think?

5. "Lennie looked sadly up at him. "They was so little," he said apologetically. "I'd pet 'em, and pretty soon they bit my fingers and I pinched their heads a little and then they was dead—because they was so little. I wish't we'd get the rabbits pretty soon, George. They ain't so little."

Why is the repetition of the word "little" significant?

6. "Guys like us, that work on ranches, are the loneliest guys in the world. They got no family. They don't belong no place. They come to a ranch an' work up a stake and then they go inta town and blow their stake, and the first thing you know they're poundin' their tail on some other ranch. They ain't got nothing to look ahead to."

Is George lonely? Does he contradict himself?

Of Mice And Men Chapter 1 Analyzing Passages Page 3

7. "[George] heard Lennie's whimpering cry and wheeled about. "Blubberin' like a baby! Jesus Christ! A big guy like you!" Lennie's lip quivered and tears started in his eyes. "Aw, Lennie!" George put his hand on Lennie's shoulder. "I ain't takin' it away jus' for meanness. That mouse ain't fresh, Lennie; and besides, you've broke it pettin' it. You get another mouse that's fresh and I'll let you keep it a little while."

Consider the word "big." How is it ironic?

8. "I wish I could put you in a cage with about a million mice an' let you have fun." His anger left him suddenly. He looked across the fire at Lennie's anguished face, and then he looked ashamedly at the flames."

What does this suggest about George's attitude toward Lennie?

Of Mice And Men Chapter 1
Reading Activity 3: Characters, Lexicon and Diction

Authors have many tools for creating characterization. Among those tools are lexicon, the words characters speak, and diction, the way characters use words to express themselves. These authorial choices affect the way readers perceive and understand characters and their motivations.

Complete the chart below, focusing on the lexicon and diction of Lennie and George. Go back and skim the text if you need to, to refresh your memory about these characters.

Speaker & Quote	Comment on the character's lexicon. (Does it convey ignorance, intelligence? Is it grammatical? Be specific.)	Comment on the character's diction. (Is it direct? Is it confident? Hesitant? Evasive? Be specific.)	What do your observations about lexicon and diction suggest about the speaker?
George: "Tastes all right," he admitted. "Don't really seem to be running, though. You never oughta drink water when it ain't running, Lennie," he said hopelessly. "You'd drink out of a gutter if you was thirsty."			
George: "Aw, Lennie!" George put his hand on Lennie's shoulder. "I ain't takin' it away jus' for meanness. That mouse ain't fresh, Lennie; and besides, you've broke it pettin' it. You get another mouse that's fresh and I'll let you keep it a little while."			

Of Mice And Men Chapter 1 Reading Activity 3: Characters, Lexicon and Diction Page 2

Speaker & Quote	Comment on the character's lexicon. (Does it convey ignorance, intelligence? Is it grammatical? Be specific.)	Comment on the character's diction. (Is it direct? Is it confident? Hesitant? Evasive? Be specific.)	What do your observations about lexicon and diction suggest about the speaker?
Lennie: "I was only foolin', George. I don't want no ketchup. I wouldn't eat no ketchup if it was right here beside me."			
Lennie: "An' live off the fatta the lan'," Lennie shouted. "An' have rabbits. Go on, George! Tell about what we're gonna have in the garden and about the rabbits in the cages and about the rain in the winter and the stove, and how thick the cream is on the milk like you can hardly cut it. Tell about that, George."			

Of Mice And Men Chapter 1: Action, Character, Decision

Write **A** (for Action) **C** (for Character) or **D** (for Decision) in the blank next to each to identify whether the passage/statement advances the action, tells us more about a character, or provokes a decision. On the lines under each question, provide a short explanation of your choice.

____ 1. Lennie dabbled his big paw in the water and wiggled his fingers so the water arose in little splashes; rings widened across the pool to the other side and came back again. Lennie watched them go. "Look, George. Look what I done."

____ 2. "Ain't a thing in my pocket," Lennie said cleverly.

____ 3. "God, you're a lot of trouble," said George. "I could get along so easy and so nice if I didn't have you on my tail. I could live so easy and maybe have a girl."

____ 4. George's hand remained outstretched imperiously. Slowly, like a terrier who doesn't want to bring a ball to its master, Lennie approached, drew back, approached again. George snapped his fingers sharply, and at the sound Lennie laid the mouse in his hand.

____ 5. "Tell you what I'll do, Lennie. First chance I get I'll give you a pup. Maybe you wouldn't kill it. That'd be better than mice. And you could pet it harder."

Of Mice And Men Chapter 1: Figurative Language

Read the following passages and determine if the passage contains a metaphor (M), simile (S) or no figurative language (NF). On the lines below, explain how the similes or metaphors create meaning in the passage.

_____1. On the sand banks the rabbits sat as quietly as little gray sculptured stones.

_____2. Behind him walked his opposite, a huge man, shapeless of face, with large, pale eyes, and wide, sloping shoulders; and he walked heavily, dragging his feet a little, the way a bear drags his paws. His arms did not swing at his sides, but hung loosely.

_____3. His huge companion dropped his blankets and flung himself down and drank from the surface of the green pool; drank with long gulps, snorting into the water like a horse.

_____4. Lennie hesitated, backed away, looked wildly at the brush line as though he contemplated running for his freedom.

_____5. "Blubberin' like a baby! Jesus Christ! A big guy like you."

Of Mice And Men Chapter 1: Elements of Fiction & Literary Devices

One of the primary motifs in the novel is rabbits. Consider the following passages and what meaning the references to rabbits creates in the novel.

1. On the sand banks the rabbits sat as quietly as little gray sculptured stones. And then from the direction of the state highway came the sound of footsteps on crisp sycamore leaves. The rabbits hurried noiselessly for cover.

Compare the movement of the rabbits to actions of George and Lennie.

2. "But you ain't gonna get in no trouble, because if you do, I won't let you tend the rabbits." How does George use the rabbits to manipulate Lennie?

3. "O.K—O.K. I'll tell ya again. I ain't got nothing to do. Might jus' as well spen' all my time tellin' you things and then you forget 'em, and I tell you again."

"Tried and tried," said Lennie, "but it didn't do no good. I remember about the rabbits, George."

"The hell with the rabbits. That's all you ever can remember is them rabbits. O.K.! Now you listen and this time you got to remember so we don't get in no trouble. You remember settin' in that gutter on Howard Street and watchin' that blackboard?"

Why is it significant that rabbits are "all [Lennie] can ever remember"? What does this suggest about Lennie?

Of Mice And Men Chapter 1: Elements of Fiction & Literary Devices Page 2

4. "Jus' wanted to feel that girl's dress—jus' wanted to pet it like it was a mouse—Well, how the hell did she know you jus' wanted to feel her dress? She jerks back and you hold on like it was a mouse. She yells and we got to hide in a irrigation ditch all day with guys lookin' for us, and we got to sneak out in the dark and get outa the country. All the time somethin' like that—all the time. I wisht I could put you in a cage with about a million mice an' let you have fun."

The chapter also includes a mention of keeping caged rabbits in a hutch. What is the connection between mice and rabbits? Between the girl's dress and rabbits? Why are they appealing to Lennie?

5. "An' live off the fatta the lan'," Lennie shouted. "An' have rabbits. Go on, George! Tell about what we're gonna have in the garden and about the rabbits in the cages and about the rain in the winter and the stove, and how thick the cream is on the milk like you can hardly cut it. Tell about that, George."

"Why'n't you do it yourself? You know all of it." "No . . . . you tell it. It ain't the same if I tell it. Go on . . . . George. How I get to tend the rabbits."

"Well," said George, "we'll have a big vegetable patch and a rabbit hutch and chickens. And when it rains in the winter, we'll just say the hell with goin' to work, and we'll build up a fire in the stove and set around it an' listen to the rain comin' down on the roof—Nuts!" He took out his pocket knife. "I ain't got time for no more." He drove his knife through the top of one of the bean cans, sawed out the top and passed the can to Lennie. Then he opened a second can. From his side pocket he brought out two spoons and passed one of them to Lennie.

How are the rabbits emblematic of this dream? What does the dream represent to Lennie and George?

Of Mice And Men Chapter 1: Elements of Fiction & Literary Devices Page 3

6. "Let's have different color rabbits, George."

"Sure we will," George said sleepily. "Red and blue and green rabbits, Lennie. Millions of 'em."

"Furry ones, George, like I seen in the fair in Sacramento." "Sure, furry ones."

What does George's exaggeration about the rabbits suggest about his actual view of the "fatta the lan'" dream?

Of Mice And Men Chapter 1: Meaning & Inferences 1

Read the passages and answer the related questions.

1. *"Then he replaced his hat, pushed himself back from the river, drew up his knees and embraced them. Lennie, who had been watching, imitated George exactly. He pushed himself back, drew up his knees, embraced them, looked over to George to see whether he had it just right. He pulled his hat down a little more over his eyes, the way George's hat was."*

Why does Lennie imitate George's mannerisms multiple times in the chapter? Why is this a regular occurrence for him?

2. *"Lennie looked timidly over to him. "George?"*
"Yeah, what ya want?"
"Where we goin', George?"
The little man jerked down the brim of his hat and scowled over at Lennie. "So you forgot that awready, did you? I gotta tell you again, do I? Jesus Christ, you're a crazy bastard!"
"I forgot," Lennie said softly. "I tried not to forget. Honest to God I did, George."
"O.K.—O.K. I'll tell ya again. I ain't got nothing to do. Might jus' as well spen' all my time tellin' you things and then you forget 'em, and I tell you again."
"Tried and tried," said Lennie, "but it didn't do no good. I remember about the rabbits, George."

Why does Lennie forget?

3. *"O.K.," said George. "An' you ain't gonna do no bad things like you done in Weed, neither." Lennie looked puzzled. "Like I done in Weed?" "Oh, so ya forgot that too, did ya? Well, I ain't gonna remind ya, fear ya do it again." A light of understanding broke on Lennie's face. "They run us outa Weed," he exploded triumphantly. "Run us out, hell," said George disgustedly. "We run. They was lookin' for us, but they didn't catch us."*

What happened in Weed? What can a reader infer that Lennie was accused of doing?

Of Mice And Men Chapter 1: Meaning & Inferences 1 Page 2

4. George put his hand on Lennie's shoulder. "I ain't takin' it away jus' for meanness. That mouse ain't fresh, Lennie; and besides, you've broke it pettin' it. You get another mouse that's fresh and I'll let you keep it a little while."

What doesn't Lennie understand about keeping the mouse? Why does he want it, yet a fake mouse is not acceptable to him?

5. Lennie sat down on the ground and hung his head dejectedly. "I don't know where there is no other mouse. I remember a lady used to give 'em to me—ever' one she got. But that lady ain't here." George scoffed. "Lady, huh? Don't even remember who that lady was. That was your own Aunt Clara. An' she stopped givin' 'em to ya. You always killed 'em."

Who is Aunt Clara? Where is she?

Of Mice And Men Chapter 1: Meaning & Inferences 2

Read the passage and answer the related questions.

A few miles south of Soledad, the Salinas River drops in close to the hillside bank and runs deep and green. The water is warm too, for it has slipped twinkling over the yellow sands in the sunlight before reaching the narrow pool. On one side of the river the golden foothill slopes curve up to the strong and rocky Gabilan Mountains, but on the valley side the water is lined with trees— willows fresh and green with every spring, carrying in their lower leaf junctures the debris of the winter's flooding; and sycamores with mottled, white, recumbent limbs and branches that arch over the pool. On the sandy bank under the trees the leaves lie deep and so crisp that a lizard makes a great skittering if he runs among them. Rabbits come out of the brush to sit on the sand in the evening, and the damp flats are covered with the night tracks of 'coons, and with the spreadpads of dogs from the ranches, and with the split-wedge tracks of deer that come to drink in the dark.

There is a path through the willows and among the sycamores, a path beaten hard by boys coming down from the ranches to swim in the deep pool, and beaten hard by tramps who come wearily down from the highway in the evening to jungle-up near water. In front of the low horizontal limb of a giant sycamore there is an ash pile made by many fires; the limb is worn smooth by men who have sat on it.

Evening of a hot day started the little wind to moving among the leaves. The shade climbed up the hills toward the top. On the sand banks the rabbits sat as quietly as little gray sculptured stones. And then from the direction of the state highway came the sound of footsteps on crisp sycamore leaves. The rabbits hurried noiselessly for cover. A stilted heron labored up into the air and pounded down river. For a moment the place was lifeless, and then two men emerged from the path and came into the opening by the green pool.

1. Is the landscape Steinbeck describes pastoral? Is it hospitable or inhospitable?

2. What evidence is there of human encroachment on nature? Why is it significant?

3. Enumerate mentions of cyclical occurrences in the passage. What are these references suggesting about time?

Of Mice And Men Chapter 1: What Is Friendship?

Chapter 1 introduces traveling companions and friends George and Lennie. Their interaction shows that they are interdependent on one another in different ways. Their friendship, however, is not without conflicts. Through characterization, motive and conflict, a larger theme of friendship emerges in the novel. Close reading of detail can uncover layers of meaning important to understanding a novel's themes. This writing assignment will explore the nature of friendship as depicted in the novel.

Using textual evidence from chapter 1, look for important but perhaps seemingly insignificant details to answer to the question "What is friendship?"

To explore the concept of friendship:

1. Identify passages and quotes which offer details about or insights into the characters' friendship. Look particularly for moments of conflict.

2. Examine the context of your quotes.

3. Consider the connotation and denotation of key phrases in your quotes.

   a. Is there conflict? How does it get resolved?
   b. Does the language suggest that the characters are equals or not equals?
   c. How do characters address one another?
   d. What qualities of friendship (loyalty, honesty) are present in the passage?
   e. Is their friendship threatened? If so, by what?

Of Mice And Men Chapter 1: What Is Friendship?

Use Your Own Knowledge

1. What does friendship mean to you?

2. What are the qualities of a good friend?

3. What are the responsibilities of a good friend?

Review the chapter and compare George and Lennie on the criteria in the middle column. List examples from the text to back up your claims.

George	Point of Comparison	Lennie
	Is he kind?	
	Is he helpful?	
	Is he loyal?	
	Is he truthful?	

Of Mice And Men Chapter 1: What Is Friendship?

Complete as many of these charts as you need to analyze all the information about friendship between George and Lennie. Find quotes from the text where conflict occurs between the characters.

Quote (and page number)	Paraphrase Quote	What is revealed about the speaker of the quote?	How does the speaker's attitude affect their friendship?

Of Mice And Men Chapter 1: Creative Analytical Writing Assignments

1. Write a flashback scene about the time that Aunt Clara gave Lennie a rubber mouse.

2. Write a scene in dialogue of a conversation between Lennie and George as they are being pursued as they flee Weed.

3. Write a paragraph that explains how George became a traveling laborer.

4. What is George's real dream, finding a nice girl? Describe it in a paragraph.

5. Define what responsibilities are inherent in friendship.

6. Imagine that you are Lennie. Describe the way you see the world.

7. Describe the relationship between George and Lennie.

8. Write a paragraph that speculates why George feels so much anger.

9. Write a campfire story that George might tell Lennie.

10. George and Lennie are essentially homeless migrant workers. Write a paragraph about ways in which they might struggle.

Of Mice And Men Chapter 1: Quick-Write Writing Assignments

1. Why is the natural setting of the landscape emphasized?

2. What is the relationship between man and nature in this chapter?

3. Is George's frustration with Lennie justified? Why?

4. What does it mean to live off "the fatta the lan'"?

5. Why is their dream to have a permanent home? What does this suggest about their lives as migrant workers?

6. Contrast the two men physically. Why is the contrast significant?

7. How are the men compared to animals? Why is the comparison significant?

8. Consider George asking Lennie to remember their camping location as a future hiding place. What do you suspect might happen?

9. Comment on Lennie's dishonesty.

10. Comment on Lennie's remorse and willingness to live in a cave.

NOTES
OF MICE AND MEN

MATERIALS: CHAPTER 2
OF MICE AND MEN

Reading Activity 1: True or False?

Reading Activity 2: Analyzing Passages

Reading Activity 3: Physical Attributes & Characterization

Reading Activity 4: Action, Character, Decision

Reading Activity 5: Figurative Language

Reading Activity 6: Elements of Fiction & Literary Devices

Reading Activity 7: Meaning and Inferences

Writing Activity 1: What Is Masculinity?

Suggested Writing Assignments

Quick-Write Assignments

NOTES
OF MICE AND MEN

Of Mice And Men Chapter 2: True or False?

Write *True* or *False* in the blank next to each statement. Below the statement, explain why you chose true or false, referencing the text to support your choices.

_____ 1. George and Lennie are cousins.

_____ 2. Candy has a little puppy.

_____ 3. Candy is a gossip.

Of Mice And Men Chapter 2 True or False? Page 2

_____ 4. George is a gossip.

_____ 5. Curley's wife is quiet and modest.

_____ 6. Slim killed some puppies.

Of Mice And Men Chapter 2 True or False? Evaluation

List Your Group's Members: Your Group's Question # _____

_____   _____   _____

_____   _____   _____

1 = No, Not At All   **2** = A Little   **3** = Some   **4** = Yes   **5** = Yes, Very Well

Evaluation of Question # ___
Does the explanation support the answer of true or false?   1 2 3 4 5
Is there good textual evidence to support the answer?   1 2 3 4 5
Is the answer clearly stated?   1 2 3 4 5
                   Total Score _____ of a possible 15 points

Evaluation of Question # ___
Does the explanation support the answer of true or false?   1 2 3 4 5
Is there good textual evidence to support the answer?   1 2 3 4 5
Is the answer clearly stated?   1 2 3 4 5
                   Total Score _____ of a possible 15 points

Evaluation of Question # ___
Does the explanation support the answer of true or false?   1 2 3 4 5
Is there good textual evidence to support the answer?   1 2 3 4 5
Is the answer clearly stated?   1 2 3 4 5
                   Total Score _____ of a possible 15 points

Evaluation of Question # ___
Does the explanation support the answer of true or false?   1 2 3 4 5
Is there good textual evidence to support the answer?   1 2 3 4 5
Is the answer clearly stated?   1 2 3 4 5
                   Total Score _____ of a possible 15 points

Evaluation of Question # ___
Does the explanation support the answer of true or false?   1 2 3 4 5
Is there good textual evidence to support the answer?   1 2 3 4 5
Is the answer clearly stated?   1 2 3 4 5
                   Total Score _____ of a possible 15 points

Copyright 2014

Of Mice And Men Chapter 2 Analyzing Passages

Answer the questions following the quotations completely.

1. "We travel together," said George coldly.
"Oh, so it's that way."
George was tense and motionless. "Yea, it's that way."

What is Curley inferring? What does Curley not quite understand?

2. "And these shelves were loaded with little articles, soap and talcum powder, razors and those Western magazines ranch men love to read and scoff at and secretly believe."

What does the contradiction about the magazines suggest about men like George?

3. "I wasn't kicked in the head with no horse, was I, George?"
"Be a damn good thing if you was," George said viciously. "Save ever'body a hell of a lot of trouble."

What are the connotations of the word "vicious," and how do they shape the reader's view of George?

4. "Well, that glove's fulla Vaseline."
"Vaseline? What the hell for?"
"Well, I will tell ya what—Curley says he's keepin' that hand soft for his wife."

What are Candy and George's reactions to this supposed fact about Curley? How does it shape their perception of him?

Of Mice And Men Chapter 2 Analyzing Passages Page 2

5. "The swamper considered… "Well . . . tell you what. Curley's like a lot of little guys. He hates big guys. He's alla time picking scraps with big guys. Kind of like he's mad at 'em because he ain't a big guy. You seen little guys like that, ain't you? Always scrappy?"

According to Candy's logic, what does "scrappy" mean? What motivates Curley to behave this way, in Candy's estimation?

6. "…he moved with a majesty only achieved by royalty and master craftsman. He was a jerkline skinner, the prince of the ranch, capable of driving ten, sixteen, even twenty mules with a single line to the leaders. He was capable of killing a fly on the wheeler's butt with a bull whip without touching the mule. There was a gravity in his manner and a quiet so profound that all talk stopped when he spoke, His authority was so great that his word was taken on any subject, be it politics or love. This was Slim, the jerkline skinner."

What is the tone of this passage? What does it suggest about masculinity?

7. "She slang her pups last night," said Slim. "Nine of 'em. I drowned four of 'em right off. She couldn't feed that many." Is this more shocking or compassionate?

What does the action of drowning the puppies suggest about Slim?

Of Mice And Men Chapter 2 Analyzing Passages Page 3

8. "Lennie's eyes moved down over her body, and though she didn't seem to be looking at Lennie she bridled a little. She looked at her fingers. "Sometimes Curley's in here," she explained. George said brusquely, "Well he ain't now."

"If he ain't, I guess I better look someplace else," she said playfully.

Lennie watched her, fascinated. George said, "If I see him, I'll pass the word you was looking for him."

She smiled archly and twitched her body. "Nobody can't blame a person for lookin'," she said. There were footsteps behind her, going by. She turned her head. "Hi, Slim," she said."

What does Curley's wife's retort ("nobody can't…") suggest about her views on marital fidelity?

Of Mice And Men Chapter 2
Reading Activity 3: Physical Attributes and Characterization

From the list of characters below, select three. Locate details about these characters' physical appearance in chapter 2. Complete the chart below using this evidence from the text. Then, after reviewing the quotes you selected, write about how these physical attributes form a clearer characterization. Use your books to locate significant details about each character's physical appearance (body, mannerisms, gestures, clothing, etc.).

Candy | Curley | Crooks | Slim | Curley' Wife

Character	Quote 1	Quote 2	Quote 3	How do quotes inform characterization?

Of Mice And Men Chapter 2: Action, Character, Decision

Write **A** (for Action) **C** (for Character) or **D** (for Decision) in the blank next to each to identify whether the passage/statement advances the action, tells us more about a character, or provokes a decision. On the lines under each question, provide a short explanation of your choice.

____ 1. But don't you try to put nothing over, Milton. I got my eye on you.

____ 2. Don't make no mistake about that. He's the boss's son. Look, Lennie. You try to keep away from him, will you? Don't never speak to him. If he comes in here you move clear to the other side of the room. Will you do that, Lennie?"

____ 3. Carlson stepped back to let Slim precede him, and then the two of them went out the door.

____ 4. "Sure," said George. "I seen plenty tough little guys. But this Curley better not make no mistakes about Lennie. Lennie ain't handy, but this Curley punk is gonna get hurt if he messes around with Lennie."

____ 5. She wore a cotton house dress and red mules, on the insteps of which were little bouquets of red ostrich feathers.

Of Mice And Men Chapter 2: Figurative Language

Read the following passages and determine if the passage contains a metaphor (M) or simile (S). On the lines below, explain how figurative language creates meaning in the passage.

____1. At about ten o'clock in the morning the sun threw a bright dust-laden bar through one of the side windows, and in and out of the beam flies shot like rushing stars.

____2. "No, he ain't, but he's sure a hell of a good worker. Strong as a bull."

____3. He was a jerkline skinner, the prince of the ranch, capable of driving ten, sixteen, even twenty mules with a single line to the leaders.

____4. His hands, large and lean, were as delicate in their action as those of a temple dancer.

____5. The curls, tiny little sausages, were spread on the hay behind her head, and her lips were parted.

Of Mice And Men Chapter 2: Elements of Fiction & Literary Devices

Read the following passages and answer questions, making inferences about the significance of symbols, motifs and themes.

1. "The old man came slowly into the room. He had his broom in his hand. And at his heels there walked a dragfooted sheepdog, gray of muzzle, and with pale, blind old eyes. The dog struggled lamely to the side of the room and lay down, grunting softly to himself and licking his grizzled, moth-eaten coat. The swamper watched him until he was settled. "I wasn't listenin'. I was jus' standin' in the shade a minute scratchin' my dog.""

How are Candy and his dog similar? Why is this significant?

2. "Carlson said thoughtfully, "Well, looka here, Slim. I been thinkin'. That dog of Candy's is so God damn old he can't hardly walk. Stinks like hell, too. Ever' time he comes into the bunk house I can smell him for two, three days. Why'n't you get Candy to shoot his old dog and give him one of the pups to raise up? I can smell that dog a mile away. Got no teeth, damn near blind, can't eat. Candy feeds him milk. He can't chew nothing else.""

Why does Carlson ask Slim to convince Candy to shoot his dog? How does Carlson justify the act?

3. "After a moment the ancient dog walked lamely in through the open door. He gazed about with mild, half-blind eyes. He sniffed, and then lay down and put his head between his paws. Curley popped into the doorway again and stood looking into the room. The dog raised his head, but when Curley jerked out, the grizzled head sank to the floor again."

a. What does Candy's dog symbolize?

Of Mice And Men Chapter 2: Elements of Fiction & Literary Devices Page 2

b. One of the major conflicts explored in this chapter is man versus the natural world. How is that theme related to Candy's dog?

c. How is the conflict of man versus the natural world related to Slim's dog, Lulu, and her pups?

Of Mice And Men Chapter 2: Meaning & Inferences 1

Read the passages and answer the related questions.

1. *""Yeah? Married two weeks and got the eye? Maybe that's why Curley's pants is full of ants."*

What does the idiom "pants is full of ants" mean here, and what is its cause?

_____
_____
_____

2. *""For two bits I'd shove out of here. If we can get jus' a few dollars in the poke we'll shove off and go up the American River and pan gold. We can make maybe a couple of dollars a day there, and we might hit a pocket."*

George consider this alternative plan when he recognizes that the ranch may be a potentially hostile place. Does he believe that it is actually possible? If so, why? If not, then why does he even mention it?

_____
_____
_____

3. *"Well, Curley's pretty handy," the swamper said skeptically. "Never did seem right to me. S'pose Curley jumps a big guy an' licks him. Ever'body says what a game guy Curley is. And s'pose he does the same thing and gets licked. Then ever'body says the big guy oughtta pick on somebody his own size, and maybe they gang up on the big guy. Never did seem right to me. Seem like Curley ain't givin' nobody a chance."*

What does "givin' nobody a chance" mean?

_____
_____
_____

4. *Slim looked through George and beyond him. "Ain't many guys travel around together," he mused. "I don't know why. Maybe ever'body in the whole damn world is scared of each other."*

What is Slim suggesting about "guys"? Why is "ever'body" significant?

_____
_____
_____

5. *George said, "Ya know, Lennie, I'm scared I'm gonna tangle with that bastard myself. I hate his guts. Jesus Christ! Come on. They won't be a damn thing left to eat."*

Why does George respond so strongly to Curley?

_____
_____
_____

Of Mice And Men Chapter 2: Meaning & Inferences 2

Read the passage and answer the related questions.

...He got married a couple of weeks ago. Wife lives over in the boss's house. Seems like Curley is cockier'n ever since he got married."
George grunted, "Maybe he's showin' off for his wife."
The swamper warmed to his gossip. "You seen that glove on his left hand?"
"Yeah. I seen it."
"Well, that glove's fulla vaseline."
"Vaseline? What the hell for?"
"Well, I tell ya what—Curley says he's keepin' that hand soft for his wife."
George studied the cards absorbedly. "That's a dirty thing to tell around," he said. The old man was reassured. He had drawn a derogatory statement from George. He felt safe now, and he spoke more confidently. "Wait'll you see Curley's wife."
George cut the cards again and put out a solitaire lay, slowly and deliberately. "Purty?" he asked casually.
"Yeah. Purty . . . . but—"
George studied his cards. "But what?"
"Well—she got the eye."
"Yeah? Married two weeks and got the eye? Maybe that's why Curley's pants is full of ants."
"I seen her give Slim the eye. Slim's a jerkline skinner. Hell of a nice fella. Slim don't need to wear no high-heeled boots on a grain team. I seen her give Slim the eye. Curley never seen it. An' I seen her give Carlson the eye."
George pretended a lack of interest. "Looks like we was gonna have fun."
The swamper stood up from his box. "Know what I think?" George did not answer. "Well, I think Curley's married . . . . a tart."

1. What is George's response to Curley's glove?

2. What does George's response suggest about his views towards sex?

3. Why does a "derogatory statement" reassure Candy?

Of Mice And Men Chapter 2: Meaning & Inferences 2 Page 2

4. What attribute is praiseworthy in Curley's wife? What does that suggest about society's view of women?

5. What is the effect of the comparison of Curley to Slim? Which is more optimally "masculine"?

Of Mice And Men Chapter 2: What Is Masculinity?

In chapters 2, masculinity as a concept is explored primarily through comparisons of Curley and Slim, as well as other minor characters.

The ways in which characters interact fuel a narrative by advancing conflict, and therefore, plot. *Of Mice and Men* is very much a novel about masculine identity, competition and status. This is apparent in how the men interact with one another.

Using textual evidence from chapter 2, look for patterns to begin formulating an answer to the question "What is masculinity?". As you develop an answer, consider how it relates to emerging conflicts and why it is significant. What do these relationship dynamics reveal about the characters? How do they define the concept of masculinity in the novel?

To determine an idea about how masculinity is defined within the novel:

1. Identify passages and quotes where Curley and Slim are described and in which they interact with other male characters.

2. Examine the context of your quotes.

3. Consider the connotation and denotation of key phrases in your quotes.

   a. What is the tone—friendly, adversarial, angry, competitive?
   b. Is there a conflict?
   c. What attitudes about masculinity are the characters revealing or concealing in their language?

4. Look for patterns in your evidence. Is a word or idea repeated? Use these patterns to shape an answer to the question.

Of Mice And Men Chapter 2: What Is Masculinity?

Complete the chart to analyze information to develop ideas to write your essay.

Character	Quote/Passage	Observations	What does it express about masculinity?
Curley Passage 1			
Curley Passage 2			
Curley Passage 3			

Slim Passage 1			
Slim Passage 2			
Slim Passage 3			

Of Mice And Men Chapter 2: What Is Masculinity?

Evaluate Your Textual Evidence

1. Are there any similarities between Curley and Slim?

2. What are the primary differences between Curley and Slim?

3. How do other people perceive each, Curley and Slim?

4. How do others perceive the masculinity of Curley and Slim? Are those perceptions positive or negative?

Of Mice And Men Chapter 2: Creative Analytical Writing Assignments

1. Write a description of George and Lennie from the boss' perspective.

2. Write a scene in dialogue of the conversation that morning between the boss and Crooks.

3. What are the "rules" of gossiping?

4. Write a letter from Curley's wife to her family who live far away.

5. Write guidelines for living in the bunkhouse.

6. Write a description of Curley's boxing career.

7. Write a scene in dialogue of the conversation between Slim and Candy about putting down Candy's dog.

8. Write a paragraph that speculates why George feels so much anger.

9. Write a flashback scene of Curley's wedding.

10. Describe how Lennie and George benefit from traveling together.

Of Mice And Men Chapter 2: Quick-Write Writing Assignments

1. Who is the better dog owner, Candy or Slim?
2. What lies does George tell? Are they justified?
3. Why is it fitting that George plays solitaire?
4. Why is the use of nicknames significant?
5. Why is Lennie "fascinated" by Curley's wife?
6. What events might be foreshadowed in this chapter?
7. How are the men compared to animals? Why is the comparison significant?
8. Consider George asking Lennie to remember their camping location as a future hiding place. What do you suspect might happen?
9. Comment on Lennie's dishonesty.
10. Comment on Lennie's remorse and willingness to live in a cave.

MATERIALS: CHAPTER 3
OF MICE AND MEN

Reading Activity 1: True or False?

Reading Activity 2: Analyzing Passages

Reading Activity 3: Foil Character Study

Reading Activity 4: Action, Character, Decision

Reading Activity 5: Figurative Language

Reading Activity 6: Elements of Fiction & Literary Devices

Reading Activity 7: Meaning and Inferences

Writing Activity 1: How Is Strength Or Weakness Determined?

Suggested Writing Assignments

Quick-Write Assignments

NOTES
OF MICE AND MEN

Of Mice And Men Chapter 3: True or False?

Write *True* or *False* in the blank next to each statement. Below the statement, explain why you chose true or false, referencing the text to support your choices.

_____ 1. Slim is impressed by Lennie's physical strength.

_____ 2. George lies to Slim about what happens in Weed.

_____ 3. George is interested in hiring a prostitute.

Of Mice And Men Chapter 3 True or False? Page 2

_____ 4. Candy already has half the money needed to buy a small farm.

_____ 5. George gives Lennie permission to hit Curley.

_____ 6. Curley accidentally mangles his hand in a machine.

Of Mice And Men Chapter 3 True or False? Evaluation

List Your Group's Members: Your Group's Question # _____

_____   _____   _____

_____   _____   _____

1 = No, Not At All **2** = A Little **3** = Some **4** = Yes **5** = Yes, Very Well

Evaluation of Question # ___
Does the explanation support the answer of true or false?   1 2 3 4 5
Is there good textual evidence to support the answer?   1 2 3 4 5
Is the answer clearly stated?   1 2 3 4 5
                            Total Score _____ of a possible 15 points

Evaluation of Question # ___
Does the explanation support the answer of true or false?   1 2 3 4 5
Is there good textual evidence to support the answer?   1 2 3 4 5
Is the answer clearly stated?   1 2 3 4 5
                            Total Score _____ of a possible 15 points

Evaluation of Question # ___
Does the explanation support the answer of true or false?   1 2 3 4 5
Is there good textual evidence to support the answer?   1 2 3 4 5
Is the answer clearly stated?   1 2 3 4 5
                            Total Score _____ of a possible 15 points

Evaluation of Question # ___
Does the explanation support the answer of true or false?   1 2 3 4 5
Is there good textual evidence to support the answer?   1 2 3 4 5
Is the answer clearly stated?   1 2 3 4 5
                            Total Score _____ of a possible 15 points

Evaluation of Question # ___
Does the explanation support the answer of true or false?   1 2 3 4 5
Is there good textual evidence to support the answer?   1 2 3 4 5
Is the answer clearly stated?   1 2 3 4 5
                            Total Score _____ of a possible 15 points

Of Mice And Men Chapter 3 Analyzing Passages

Answer the questions following the quotations completely.

1. George carefully built his line of solitaire cards. "Well, that girl rabbits in an' tells the law she been raped. The guys in Weed start a party out to lynch Lennie.

So we sit in a irrigation ditch under water all the rest of that day. Got on'y our heads sticking outa water, an' up under the grass that sticks out from the side of the ditch. An' that night we scrammed outa there."

What does the word "rabbits" probably mean here? Why is it significant?

2. The skinner had been studying the old dog with his calm eyes. "Yeah," he said. "You can have a pup if you want to." He seemed to shake himself free for speech. "Carl's right, Candy. That dog ain't no good to himself. I wisht somebody'd shoot me if I get old an' a cripple."

Why is the word "cripple" significant? Why is it significant that Slim says this to Candy?

3. Whit laid down his cards impressively. "Well, stick around an' keep your eyes open. You'll see plenty. She ain't concealin' nothing. I never seen nobody like her. She got the eye goin' all the time on everybody. I bet she even gives the stable buck the eye. I don't know what the hell she wants."

What references are made to eyes here? What does this suggest about eyes and seeing? How does gender factor in?

4. They fell into a silence. They looked at one another, amazed. This thing they had never really believed in was coming true. George said reverently, "Jesus Christ! I bet we could swing her." His eyes were full of wonder. "I bet we could swing her," he repeated softly.

What is happening with pronouns here? What does that suggest about George's view of the world?

Of Mice And Men Chapter 3 Analyzing Passages Page 2

5. Slim said, "Well, you been askin' me too often. I'm gettin' God damn sick of it. If you can't look after your own God damn wife, what you expect me to do about it? You lay offa me."

What is Slim suggesting that Curley is implying? Why is the repetition of "God damn" significant?

6. Carlson laughed. "You God damn punk," he said. "You tried to throw a scare into Slim, an' you couldn't make it stick. Slim throwed a scare into you. You're yella as a frog belly. I don't care if you're the best welter in the country. You come for me, an' I'll kick your God damn head off."

Why is Carlson emboldened? What is Carlson suggesting about power and authority?

7. Lennie covered his face with his huge paws and bleated with terror. He cried, "Make 'um stop, George." Then Curley attacked his stomach and cut off his wind.

What is the significance of the animal imagery? Does it make Lennie seem more forceful or less?

8. George turned to Lennie. "It ain't your fault," he said. "You don't need to be scairt no more. You done jus' what I tol' you to. Maybe you better go in the wash room an' clean up your face. You look like hell.

Does George accept responsibility for Lennie's actions? How is that conveyed in the text?

Of Mice And Men Chapter 3 Reading Activity 3: Foil Character Study

Complete the chart below with quotes from the text and inferences about Lennie and Curley. Consider how Curley's attributes and actions provide insight into Lennie's character.

Incident	Quotes/Phrases	What does this show about Curley?	What does this show about Lennie?
When George questions Lennie about seeing Curley's wife in the barn			
When Curley asks Lennie what he is laughing at			
When Curley strikes Lennie			
When Lennie is holding and damaging Curley's hand			

Of Mice And Men Chapter 3: Action, Character, Decision

Write **A** (for Action) **C** (for Character) or **D** (for Decision) in the blank next to each to identify whether the passage/statement advances the action, tells us more about a character, or provokes a decision. On the lines under each question, provide a short explanation of your choice.

___ 1. "Well, I can't stand him in here," said Carlson. "That stink hangs around even after he's gone." He walked over with his heavy-legged stride and looked down at the dog. "Got no teeth," he said. "He's all stiff with rheumatism. He ain't no good to you, Candy. An' he ain't no good to himself. Why'n't you shoot him, Candy?"

___ 2. Candy looked for help from face to face.

___ 3. Then he said thoughtfully, "Look, if me an' Lennie work a month an' don't spen' nothing, we'll have a hunderd bucks. That'd be four fifty. I bet we could swing her for that. Then you an' Lennie could go get her started an' I'd get a job an' make up the res', an' you could sell eggs an' stuff like that."

___ 4. "I ought to of shot that dog myself, George. I shouldn't ought to of let no stranger shoot my dog."

___ 5. Lennie was still smiling with delight at the memory of the ranch.

Of Mice And Men Chapter 3: Figurative Language

Read the following passages and determine if the passage contains hyperbole (H) or understatement (U). On the lines below, explain how figurative language creates meaning in the passage.

_____1. Maybe we'd have a cow or a goat, and the cream is so God damn thick you got to cut it with a knife and take it out with a spoon.

_____2. "We could live offa the fatta the lan'."

_____3. "It wasn't nothing," said Slim. "I would of had to drowned most of 'em anyways. No need to thank me about that."

_____4. That's right. You couldn't find it in a hundred years.

_____5. You jus' let 'em try to get the rabbits. I'll break their God damn necks. I'll . . . . I'll smash 'em with a stick." He subsided, grumbling to himself, threatening the future cats which might dare to disturb the future rabbits.

Of Mice And Men Chapter 3: Elements of Fiction & Literary Devices

Read the following passages and answer questions, making inferences about the significance of symbols, motifs and themes.

1. "Although there was evening brightness showing through the windows of the bunk house, inside it was dusk."

The chapter opens with a reference to a motif of darkness, which is repeated multiple times through the chapter. What is the effect of the motif?

2. "George looked over at Slim and saw the calm, Godlike eyes fastened on him."

The description of Slim's eyes as "Godlike" suggests what about him?

3. George said, "You get right up an' take this pup back to the nest. He's gotta sleep with his mother. You want to kill him? Just born last night an' you take him out of the nest. You take him back or I'll tell Slim not to let you have him."

How does this example fit with a larger theme of protecting the weak?

4. "It was obvious that Whit was not interested in his cards. He laid his hand down and George scooped it in. George laid out his deliberate solitaire hand—seven cards and six on top, and five on top of those."

How does the failed euchre game with Whit relate to the theme of companionship/isolation?

Of Mice And Men Chapter 3: Elements of Fiction & Literary Devices Page 2

5. "...Susy's got nice chairs to set in, too. If a guy don't want a flop, why he can just set in the chairs and have a couple or three shots and pass the time of day and Susy don't give a damn. She ain't rushin' guys through and kickin' 'em out if they don't want a flop...."

...

"Me an' Lennie's rollin' up a stake," said George. "I might go in an' set and have a shot, but I ain't puttin' out no two and a half."

...

George sighed. "You give me a good whore house every time," he said. "A guy can go in an' get drunk and get ever'thing outta his system all at once, an' no messes. And he knows how much it's gonna set him back. There here jail baits is just set on the trigger of the hoosegow."

Consider Whit's description of whorehouses and George's response, as well as George's reminder to Lennie about Andy Cushman. What is being suggested by the text about women?

_____
_____
_____
_____

Of Mice and Men Chapter 3: Meaning & Inferences 1

Read the passages and answer the related questions.

1. George said, "She's gonna make a mess. They's gonna be a bad mess about her. She's a jail bait all set on the trigger. That Curley got his work cut out for him. Ranch with a bunch of guys on it ain't no place for a girl, specially like her."

What does "mess" mean in the passage? Do both uses have the same meaning?

_____
_____
_____

2. Curley looked threateningly about the room. "Where the hell's Slim?"
"Went out in the barn," said George. "He was gonna put some tar on a split hoof."
Curley's shoulders dropped and squared. "How long ago'd he go?"

Why is the mention of Curley's shoulders significant?

_____
_____
_____

3. ...We'd have a setter dog and a couple stripe cats, but you gotta watch out them cats don't get the little rabbits."
Lennie breathed hard. "You jus' let 'em try to get the rabbits. I'll break their God damn necks. I'll . . . . I'll smash 'em with a stick." He subsided, grumbling to himself, threatening the future cats which might dare to disturb the future rabbits.

Does Lennie mean what he says?

_____
_____
_____

Of Mice And Men Chapter 3: Meaning & Inferences 1 Page 2

4. *"You seen what they done to my dog tonight? They says he wasn't no good to himself nor nobody else. When they can me here I wisht somebody'd shoot me. But they won't do nothing like that. I won't have no place to go, an' I can't get no more jobs.*

In what ways is Candy identifying with his dog?

_____
_____
_____
_____
_____

5. *Slim smiled wryly. He knelt down beside Curley. "You got your senses in hand enough to listen?" he asked. Curley nodded. "Well, then listen," Slim went on. "I think you got your han' caught in a machine. If you don't tell nobody what happened, we ain't going to. But you jus' tell an' try to get this guy canned and we'll tell ever'body, an' then will you get the laugh."*

How is the use of the idiom "in hand" ironic here?

_____
_____
_____
_____

Of Mice And Men Chapter 3: Meaning & Inferences 2

Read the passage and answer the related questions.

George looked over at Slim and saw the calm, Godlike eyes fastened on him. "Funny," said George. "I used to have a hell of a lot of fun with 'im. Used to play jokes on 'im 'cause he was too dumb to take care of 'imself. But he was too dumb even to know he had a joke played on him. I had fun. Made me seem God damn smart alongside of him. Why he'd do any damn thing I tol' him. If I tol' him to walk over a cliff, over he'd go. That wasn't so damn much fun after a while. He never got mad about it, neither. I've beat the hell outa him, and he coulda bust every bone in my body jus' with his han's, but he never lifted a finger against me." George's voice was taking on the tone of confession. "Tell you what made me stop that. One day a bunch of guys was standin' around up on the Sacramento River. I was feelin' pretty smart. I turns to Lennie and says, 'Jump in.' An' he jumps. Couldn't swim a stroke. He damn near drowned before we could get him. An' he was so damn nice to me for pullin' him out. Clean forgot I told him to jump in. Well, I ain't done nothing like that no more."

1. How has George's treatment of Lennie changed over time?

2. What is George's tone in the passage? What does that suggest about his morality?

3. What words in the passage are synonyms for intelligence? Are they positively or negatively connoted?

4. What does George suggest about power and authority in their relationship?

5. What is the effect of Lennie's response to being saved from drowning on George?

Of Mice and Men Chapter 3: How Is Weakness Or Strength Determined?

In chapter 3, weakness and strength are concepts interrogated by the physical confrontation that occurs between Curley and Lennie.

In the novel, though, the concepts are presented in a paradoxical way. For example, Lennie, who is physically imposing, has the last name "small." Curley, a former boxer who is constantly looking to tussle with someone, is physically small in stature. This paradoxical presentation calls into question what the qualities of weakness and strength are.

Using textual evidence from Chapter 3, look for patterns to begin formulating an answer to the question "How is weakness or strength determined?". In what ways do Steinbeck's characters subvert expectations about what it usually means to be weak or strong?

To formulate an idea about how weakness or strength is determined:

1. Identify passages and quotes from the scene which describes Lennie and Curley's physical altercation.

2. Examine the context of your quotes.

3. Consider the connotation and denotation of key phrases in your quotes.

    a. What is the tone—is it aggressive, complacent, scared?
    b. Is there a conflict?
    c. How do other characters react, and what do their reactions suggest about strength and weakness?

4. Look for patterns in your evidence. Is a word or idea repeated? Use these patterns to shape an answer to the question.

Of Mice And Men Chapter 3: How Is Weakness Or Strength Determined? Page 2

Complete the chart to analyze information to develop ideas to write your essay.

Incident	Quote/Passage	Observations	What does it express about strength or weakness—physically or morally?
Curley picks fight with Lennie			
Lennie is frightened			
Lennie hurts Curley			

Of Mice And Men Chapter 3: How Is Weakness Or Strength Determined? Page 3

Incident	Quote/Passage	Observations	What does it express about strength or weakness—physically or morally?
Other characters respond			
Lennie tries to make sense of what happened			

Of Mice And Men Chapter 3: How Is Weakness Or Strength Determined? Page 4

A. Evaluate Your Textual Evidence

1. What motivates Curley?

2. Is Lennie's resistance to fighting a sign of weakness or strength?

3. How do other people perceive Curley and Lennie—is one weaker or stronger?

4. How do Curley and Lennie challenge conventional definitions of weakness and strength?

B. Make Notes About Your Conclusions

Of Mice and Men Chapter 3: Creative Analytical Writing Assignments

1. Write the story of Candy's dog, recalling its vitality and youth.

2. Imagine you are George. Why do you like to play solitaire?

3. Write dialogue of what you think Candy should have said when Slim agreed with Carlson over the old dog's fate.

4. Write a narrative description of Candy's shooting of the dog.

5. As Curley was overpowered during his altercation with Lennie, what might Curley have been thinking?

6. Write a flashback scene about the time George's cruelty toward Lennie almost caused Lennie to drown.

7. Write a stream-of-consciousness from Curley's point of view in which he admits why he feels self-conscious and inferior to others.

8. Describe what it might have been like for George and Lennie to hide in the irrigation ditch.

9. Write a flashback scene of George meeting Lennie.

10. Write a letter to the magazine editor expressing how the articles give ranch hands a feeling of hope and community.

Of Mice and Men Chapter 3: Quick-Write Writing Assignments

1. Is Lennie like George's pet in some ways? How?
2. Compare the brothels described. Why is one preferred over the other?
3. Is Carlson right about the dog?
4. What does Candy fear?
5. Why is it significant that George mentions his "stake" so many times?
6. Why does Slim have so much moral authority?
7. Does Curley get what he deserves?
8. Why is Lennie so upset by the physical altercation?
9. Is George's earlier poor treatment of Lennie surprising?
10. What "foreshadows" from earlier chapters have already transpired?

MATERIALS: CHAPTER 4
OF MICE AND MEN

Reading Activity 1: True or False?

Reading Activity 2: Analyzing Passages

Reading Activity 3: Direct vs. Indirect Characterization

Reading Activity 4: Action, Character, Decision

Reading Activity 5: Figurative Language

Reading Activity 6: Elements of Fiction & Literary Devices

Reading Activity 7: Meaning and Inferences

Writing Activity 1: What Are The Effects Of Isolation?

Suggested Writing Assignments

Quick-Write Assignments

NOTES
OF MICE AND MEN

Of Mice And Men Chapter 4: True or False?

Write *True* or *False* in the blank next to each statement. Below the statement, explain why you chose true or false, referencing the text to support your choices.

_____ 1. Lennie is unaware of racism.

_____ 2. Crooks suffers from chronic pain from his crooked spine.

_____ 3. Crooks is protective and caring toward Lennie.

Of Mice And Men Chapter 4 True or False? Page 2

_____ 4. Crooks dislikes being alone because he cannot ask someone else if they also saw or experienced something unusual.

_____ 5. Curley's wife had a successful career as a theater actress

_____ 6. Curley's wife believes that if she accused Crooks of violence toward her that he would be killed.

Of Mice And Men Chapter 4 True or False? Evaluation

List Your Group's Members: Your Group's Question # _____

_____   _____   _____

_____   _____   _____

1 = No, Not At All **2** = A Little **3** = Some **4** = Yes **5** = Yes, Very Well

Evaluation of Question # ___
Does the explanation support the answer of true or false?	1 2 3 4 5
Is there good textual evidence to support the answer?	1 2 3 4 5
Is the answer clearly stated?	1 2 3 4 5

Total Score _____ of a possible 15 points

Evaluation of Question # ___
Does the explanation support the answer of true or false?	1 2 3 4 5
Is there good textual evidence to support the answer?	1 2 3 4 5
Is the answer clearly stated?	1 2 3 4 5

Total Score _____ of a possible 15 points

Evaluation of Question # ___
Does the explanation support the answer of true or false?	1 2 3 4 5
Is there good textual evidence to support the answer?	1 2 3 4 5
Is the answer clearly stated?	1 2 3 4 5

Total Score _____ of a possible 15 points

Evaluation of Question # ___
Does the explanation support the answer of true or false?	1 2 3 4 5
Is there good textual evidence to support the answer?	1 2 3 4 5
Is the answer clearly stated?	1 2 3 4 5

Total Score _____ of a possible 15 points

Evaluation of Question # ___
Does the explanation support the answer of true or false?	1 2 3 4 5
Is there good textual evidence to support the answer?	1 2 3 4 5
Is the answer clearly stated?	1 2 3 4 5

Total Score _____ of a possible 15 points

Of Mice And Men Chapter 4 Analyzing Passages

Answer the questions following the quotations completely.

1. "...You go on get outta my room. I ain't wanted in the bunk house, and you ain't wanted in my room."
"Why ain't you wanted?" Lennie asked.
"'Cause I'm black..."

Why is the repetition of "ain't" significant?

2. "George can tell you screwy things, and it don't matter It's just the talking. It's just bein' with another guy. That's all."

Why is talking important to Crooks?

3. ""You're nuts." Crooks was scornful. "I seen hunderds of men come by on the road an' on the ranches, with their bindles on their back an' that same damn thing in their heads. Hunderds of them. They come, an' they quit an' go on; an' every damn one of 'em's got a little piece of land in his head. An' never a God damn one of 'em ever gets it. Just like heaven. Ever'body wants a little piece of lan'. I read plenty of books out here. Nobody never gets to heaven, and nobody gets no land. It's just in their head. They're all the time talkin' about it, but it's jus' in their head."

What is Crooks comparing "heaven" to? Is it attainable?

Of Mice And Men Chapter 4 Analyzing Passages Page 2

4. Candy leaned against the wall beside the broken collar while he scratched his wrist stump. "I been here a long time," he said. "An' Crooks been here a long time. This's the first time I ever been in his room."

What is the significance of the details in the passage, particularly the "broken collar" and "wrist stump"?

5. Well, you keep your place then, Nigger. I could get you strung up on a tree so easy it ain't even funny."

Crooks had reduced himself to nothing. There was no personality, no ego—nothing to arouse either like or dislike. He said, "Yes, ma'am," and his voice was toneless.

In what ways does Crooks change? What prompts this?

6. The stable buck went on dreamily, "I remember when I was little kid on my old man's chicken ranch. Had two brothers. They was always near me, always there. Used to sleep right in the same room, right in the same bed—all three. Had a strawberry patch. Had an alfalfa patch. Used to turn the chickens out in the alfalfa on a sunny morning. My brothers'd set on a fence rail an' watch 'em—white chickens they was."

Compare Crooks' nostalgic memories to his current situation.

Of Mice And Men Chapter 4 Analyzing Passages Page 3

7. Candy said, "That bitch didn't ought to of said that to you."

"It wasn't nothing," Crooks said dully. "You guys comin' in an' settin' made me forget. What she says is true."

Do Candy and Crooks share the same outlook on Curley's wife?

8. "Awright," she said contemptuously. "Awright, cover 'im up if ya wanta. Whatta I care? You bindle bums think you're so damn good. Whatta ya think I am, a kid? I tell ya I could of went with shows. Not jus' one, neither. An' a guy tol' me he could put me in pitchers…" She was breathless with indignation. "—Sat'iday night. Ever'body out doin' som'pin'. Ever'body! An' what am I doin'? Standin' here talkin' to a bunch of bindle stiffs—a nigger an' a dum-dum and a lousy ol' sheep—an' likin' it because they ain't nobody else."

What is causing Curley's wife's "indignation" and anger?

Of Mice And Men Chapter 4
Reading Activity 3: Direct vs. Indirect Characterization

Characterization, or the development of characters in a work of fiction, can be direct or indirect. Direct characterization is revealing aspects of character directly to the reader via a narrator, the character him or herself or from another character. Indirect characterization requires readers to infer what a character is like through the character's thoughts, action, diction, appearance and interactions with others.

Complete the chart, using actual quotes when asked and noting page numbers.

Character	Direct Characterization Quote	Indirect Characterization Quote	Indirect Characterization Inference
Crooks			
Lennie			
Candy			
Curley's wife			

Of Mice and Men Chapter 4: Action, Character, Decision

Write **A** (for Action) **C** (for Character) or **D** (for Decision) in the blank next to each to identify whether the passage/statement advances the action, tells us more about a character, or provokes a decision. On the lines under each question, provide a short explanation of your choice.

____ 1. Crooks possessed several pairs of shoes, a pair of rubber boots, a big alarm clock and a single-barreled shotgun. And he had books, too; a tattered dictionary and a mauled copy of the California civil code for 1905. There were battered magazines and a few dirty books on a special shelf over his bunk. A pair of large gold-rimmed spectacles hung from a nail on the wall above his bed.

____ 2. Crooks scowled, but Lennie's disarming smile defeated him. "Come on in and set a while," Crooks said. "'Long as you won't get out and leave me alone, you might as well set down."

____ 3. "I said s'pose George went into town tonight and you never heard of him no more." Crooks pressed forward some kind of private victory. "Just s'pose that," he repeated.

____ 4. Candy's face had grown redder and redder, but before she was done speaking, he had control of himself. He was the master of the situation. "I might of knew," he said gently. "Maybe you just better go along an' roll your hoop. We ain't got nothing to say to you at all. We know what we got, and we don't care whether you know it or not. So maybe you better jus' scatter along now, 'cause Curley maybe ain't gonna like his wife out in the barn with us 'bindle stiffs.'"

____ 5. "Well, jus' forget it," said Crooks. "I didn't mean it. Jus' foolin'. I wouldn' want to go no place like that."

Of Mice And Men Chapter 4: Figurative Language

Read the following passages, and determine if the language is figurative (F) or literal (L). On the lines below, explain any use of figurative language and the effect it has on meaning.

_____1. "You're nuts," said Crooks. "You're crazy as a wedge. What rabbits you talkin' about?"

_____2. "George can tell you screwy things, and it don't matter. It's just the talking. It's just bein' with another guy. That's all."

_____3. Crooks bored in on him. "Want me ta tell ya what'll happen? They'll take ya to the booby hatch. They'll tie ya up with a collar, like a dog."

_____4. "A guy goes nuts if he ain't got nobody."

_____5. "I seen guys nearly crazy with loneliness for land, but ever' time a whore house or a blackjack game took what it takes."

Of Mice And Men Chapter 4: Elements of Fiction & Literary Devices

One of the primary themes in the novel is fear. Consider the following passages and how Steinbeck presents and defines the concept of fear.

1. Crooks saw the danger as it approached him. He edged back on his bunk to get out of the way. "I was just supposin'," he said. "George ain't hurt. He's all right. He'll be back all right."

What is Crooks afraid of here? How has presenting a hypothetical situation put him in danger?

2. ...Maybe if he sees somethin', he don't know whether it's right or not. He can't turn to some other guy and ast him if he sees it too. He can't tell. He got nothing to measure by. I seen things out here. I wasn't drunk. I don't know if I was asleep. If some guy was with me, he could tell me I was asleep, an' then it would be all right. But I jus' don't know." Crooks was looking across the room now, looking toward the window.

What is Crooks afraid of in this passage? What is the relationship between talking and fear, according to Crooks?

3. "She regarded them amusedly. "Funny thing," she said. "If I catch any one man, and he's alone, I get along fine with him. But just let two of the guys get together an' you won't talk. Jus' nothing but mad." She dropped her fingers and put her hands on her hips. "You're all scared of each other, that's what. Ever' one of you's scared the rest is goin' to get something on you."

What is Curley's wife suggesting that the men on the ranch are afraid of?

4. Maybe there was a time when we was scared of gettin' canned, but we ain't no more. We got our own lan', and it's ours, an' we c'n go to it."

What, according to Candy, has allayed the men's fear of being fired?

5. Crooks seemed to come slowly out of the layers of protection he had put on.

What are the "layers of protection," and why has Crooks protected himself?

6. "'Member what I said about hoein' and doin' odd jobs?"
"Yeah," said Candy. "I remember."
"Well, jus' forget it," said Crooks. "I didn't mean it. Jus' foolin'. I wouldn' want to go no place like that."

How does Crooks's changing his mind relate to fear?

Of Mice And Men Chapter 4: Meaning & Inferences 1

Read the passages and answer the related questions.

1. *"I was born right here in California. My old man had a chicken ranch, 'bout ten acres. The white kids come to play at our place, an' sometimes I went to play with them, and some of them was pretty nice. My ol' man didn't like that. I never knew till long later why he didn't like that. But I know now." He hesitated, and when he spoke again his voice was softer. "There wasn't another colored family for miles around. And now there ain't a colored man on this ranch an' there's jus' one family in Soledad."*

What didn't Crooks's father like? What did Crooks later understand?

2. *"The stable buck went on dreamily, "I remember when I was a little kid on my old man's chicken ranch. Had two brothers. They was always near me, always there. Used to sleep right in the same room, right in the same bed- all three. Had a strawberry patch. Had an alfalfa patch. Used to turn the chickens out in the alfalfa on a sunny morning. My brothers'd set on a fence rail an' watch 'em- white chickens they was."*

Why is "dreamily" significant? How do Crooks's memories compare to Lennie's dreams for the future?

3. *"Candy came in, but he was still embarrassed, "You got a nice cozy little place in here," he said to Crooks. "Must be nice to have a room all to yourself this way."*
"Sure," said Crooks. "And a manure pile under the window. Sure, it's swell."

Is Crooks's retort justified? Why or why not?

4. *Crooks reached around and explored his spine with his hand. "I never seen a guy really do it," he said. "I seen guys nearly crazy with loneliness for land, but ever' time a whore house or a blackjack game took what it takes." He hesitated. "...If you... guys would want a hand to work for nothing- just his keep, why I'd come an' lend a hand.*

Consider the context of the passage. What changes Crooks's mind, and how is the word "loneliness" significant in that change?

5. *"She stood still in the doorway, smiling a little at them, rubbing the nails of one hand with the thumb and forefinger of the other. And her eyes traveled from one face to another. "They left all the weak ones here," she said finally. "Think I don't know where they all went? Even Curley. I know where they all went."*

What does she mean by "weak ones"?

Of Mice And Men Chapter 4: Meaning & Inferences 2

Read the passage and answer the related questions.

The girl flared up. "Sure I gotta husban'. You all seen him. Swell guy, ain't he? Spends all his time sayin' what he's gonna do to guys he don't like, and he don't like nobody. Think I'm gonna stay in that two-by-four house and listen how Curley's gonna lead with his left twice, and then bring in the ol' right cross? 'One-two,' he says. 'Jus' the ol' one-two an' he'll go down.'" She paused and her face lost its sullenness and grew interested. "Say- what happened to Curley's han'?"

There was an embarrassed silence. Candy stole a look at Lennie. Then he coughed. "Why... Curley... he got his han' caught in a machine, ma'am. Bust his han'."

She watched for a moment, and then she laughed. "Baloney! What you think you're sellin' me? Curley started som'pin' he didn' finish. Caught in a machine- baloney! Why, he ain't give nobody the good ol' one-two since he got his han' bust. Who bust him?"

Candy repeated sullenly, "Got it caught in a machine."

"Awright," she said contemptuously. "Awright, cover 'im up if ya wanta. Whatta I care? You bindle bums think you're so damn good. Whatta ya think I am, a kid? I tell ya I could of went with shows. Not jus' one, neither. An' a guy tol' me he could put me in pitchers...." She was breathless with indignation. "-Sat'iday night. Ever'body out doin' som'pin'. Ever'body! An' what am I doin'? Standin' here talkin' to a bunch of bindle stiffs- a nigger an' a dum-dum and a lousy ol' sheep- an' likin' it because they ain't nobody else."

1. What is Curley's wife's main criticism of her husband?

2. Why is it significant that Curley's wife and Candy are both described as "sullen"?

3. In what ways does Curley's wife suggest that she is considered as less than?

4. Why does Curley's wife insult the men?

5. What is Curley's wife really indignant about?

Of Mice And Men Chapter 4: What Are The Effects Of Isolation?

Chapter 4 shows the interactions between the novel's most disempowered, oppressed and "othered" characters. While the characters' experiences might give them a sense of empathy for one another, this is not what occurs, and the chapter ends with the barriers created by class, race, gender, and physical/mental disability intact. Each of these characters remains essentially isolated from each other and the others on the ranch. This writing assignment will explore the ideas of loneliness and isolation as a product of prejudice as depicted in the novel.

Using textual evidence from Chapter 4, look for important but perhaps seemingly insignificant details to answer to the question: What are the effects of isolation?

To explore the concept of isolation:

1. Identify passages and quotes which offer details about or insights into the characters' alienation/isolation/loneliness.

2. Examine the context of your quotes.

3. Consider the connotation and denotation of key phrases in your quotes.

    a. How does the character identify or speak about his/her alienation/isolation?
    b. In what ways do characters attempt to overcome this alienation?
    c. In what ways are characters prejudiced towards one another?
    d. How do characters address one another?
    e. Why do they lack empathy for one another? How is this an effect of isolation?

Of Mice And Men Chapter 4: What Are The Effects Of Isolation? Page 2

Use Your Own Knowledge

1. What does isolation/loneliness mean to you?

2. Why are people prejudiced toward one another?

3. What are some effects of being isolated from others?

Of Mice And Men Chapter 4: What Are The Effects Of Isolation? Page 3

Complete as many of these charts as you need to analyze all the information about loneliness, isolation and alienation. Find quotes from the text where characters reveal the effects of their isolation.

Quote (and page number)	Paraphrase Quote	What is revealed about the speaker of the quote?	How is isolation affecting the speaker?

Of Mice And Men Chapter 4: Creative Analytical Writing Assignments

1. Write a flashback scene about Crooks's childhood.

2. Write a scene in dialogue of a conversation between Curley's wife and her friends about her desire to become a movie star.

3. Write a letter from Crooks to his brother that tells about his life on the ranch.

4. What is George's real dream, finding a nice girl? Describe it in a paragraph.

5. Write about ways in which Lennie would be lonely or isolated if George deserted him.

6. Write a letter from Curley's wife to her friend that describes her feelings about her marriage to Curley.

7. Describe the joy the men feel in sharing a dream to start a farm together.

8. Write about what Crooks might have seen, but could not believe his eyes.

9. Rewrite the dialogue as if the men admitted that Lennie broke Curley's hand.

10. Write a paragraph from Lennie's perspective about why he likes rabbits so much.

Of Mice and Men Chapter 4: Quick-Write Writing Assignments

1. Compare Crooks's bunk to the others' bunk.

2. Why does Curley's wife say she is thinking of getting pet rabbits?

3. Are Candy's insults toward Curley's wife justified?

4. Why is it significant that Crooks has more possessions than the others?

5. Why does Curley's wife say she likes talking to Candy, Crooks, and Lennie?

6. Does Candy believe that his word would prevail against Curley's wife about framing Crooks? Why?

7. What is the significance of the mentions of the horses and halters throughout the chapter?

8. In what ways does George act prejudiced?

9. Why is George so angry at the end of the chapter?

10. What do the mentions of Crooks's physical pain signify? Why does the chapter end with an allusion to his physical pain?

NOTES
OF MICE AND MEN

MATERIALS: CHAPTER 5
OF MICE AND MEN

Reading Activity 1: True or False?

Reading Activity 2: Analyzing Passages

Reading Activity 3: Round Characters Or Stereotypes?

Reading Activity 4: Action, Character, Decision

Reading Activity 5: Figurative Language

Reading Activity 6: Elements of Fiction & Literary Devices

Reading Activity 7: Meaning and Inferences

Writing Activity 1: What Does Curley's Wife Symbolize?

Suggested Writing Assignments

Quick-Write Assignments

NOTES
OF MICE AND MEN

Of Mice And Men Chapter 5: True or False?

Write *True* or *False* in the blank next to each statement. Below the statement, explain why you chose true or false, referencing the text to support your choices.

_____ 1. Lennie decides to tell George that he found the puppy dead.

_____ 2. Lennie talks easily and freely with Curley's wife.

_____ 3. Curley's wife longs for a different life.

Of Mice And Men Chapter 5 True or False? Page 2

_____ 4. Lennie breaks Curley's wife's neck.

_____ 5. George always believed that he could buy a farm.

_____ 6. George is afraid that he will be implicated in the death of Curley's wife.

Of Mice And Men Chapter 5 True or False? Evaluation

List Your Group's Members: Your Group's Question # _____

_____   _____   _____

_____   _____   _____

1 = No, Not At All **2** = A Little **3** = Some **4** = Yes **5** = Yes, Very Well

Evaluation of Question # ___
Does the explanation support the answer of true or false?   1 2 3 4 5
Is there good textual evidence to support the answer?   1 2 3 4 5
Is the answer clearly stated?   1 2 3 4 5
                        Total Score _____ of a possible 15 points

Evaluation of Question # ___
Does the explanation support the answer of true or false?   1 2 3 4 5
Is there good textual evidence to support the answer?   1 2 3 4 5
Is the answer clearly stated?   1 2 3 4 5
                        Total Score _____ of a possible 15 points

Evaluation of Question # ___
Does the explanation support the answer of true or false?   1 2 3 4 5
Is there good textual evidence to support the answer?   1 2 3 4 5
Is the answer clearly stated?   1 2 3 4 5
                        Total Score _____ of a possible 15 points

Evaluation of Question # ___
Does the explanation support the answer of true or false?   1 2 3 4 5
Is there good textual evidence to support the answer?   1 2 3 4 5
Is the answer clearly stated?   1 2 3 4 5
                        Total Score _____ of a possible 15 points

Evaluation of Question # ___
Does the explanation support the answer of true or false?   1 2 3 4 5
Is there good textual evidence to support the answer?   1 2 3 4 5
Is the answer clearly stated?   1 2 3 4 5
                        Total Score _____ of a possible 15 points

Of Mice And Men Chapter 5 Analyzing Passages

Answer the questions following the quotations completely.

1. He was so little," said Lennie. "I was jus playin' with him... an' he made like he's gonna bite me... an' I made like I was gonna smack him ... an'... an' I done it. An' then he was dead.

She consoled him. "Don't you worry none. He was jus' a mutt. You can get another one easy. The whole country is fulla mutts."

What is the connotation of the last line?

2. "I tell you I ain't used to livin' like this. I coulda made somethin' of myself." She said darkly, "Maybe I will yet." And then her words tumbled out in a passion of communication, as though she hurried before her listener could be taken away. "I lived right in Salinas," she said. "Come there when I was a kid. Well, a show come through, an' I met one of the actors. He says I could go with that show. But my ol' lady wouldn' let me. She says because I was on'y fifteen. But the guy says I coulda. If I'd went, I wouldn't be livin' like this, you bet."

How is Curley's wife's manner of speaking described? Why is that significant?

3. Lennie went back and looked at the dead girl. The puppy lay close to her. Lennie picked it up. "I'll throw him away," he said. "It's bad enough like it is."

What does this suggest about Lennie's capacity to understand what has happened?

Of Mice And Men Chapter 5 Analyzing Passages Page 2

4. "Then—it's all off?" Candy asked sulkily. George didn't answer his question. George said, "I'll work my month an' I'll take my fifty bucks an' I'll stay all night in some lousy cat house. Or I'll set in some poolroom til ever'body goes home. An' then I'll come back an' work another month an' I'll have fifty bucks more."

What does George's response imply?

5. Slim sighed. "Well, I guess we got to get him…"

What is the tone of Slim's statement?

6. "If we could keep Curley in, we might, But Curley's gonna want to shoot 'im. Curley's still mad about his hand. An' s'pose they lock him up an' strap him down and put him in a cage. That ain't no good, George."

According to Slim, what are the biggest threats that face Lennie?

7. And when they were gone, Candy squatted down in the hay and watched the face of Curley's wife. "Poor bastard," he said softly.

To whom is Candy referring?

Of Mice And Men Chapter 5 Analyzing Passages Page 3

8. George said softly, "—I think I knowed from the very first. I think I knowed we'd never do her. He usta like to hear about it so much I got to thinking maybe we would."

What made George believe in the dream?

Of Mice And Men Chapter 5
Reading Activity 3: Round Characters or Stereotypes

Characterization in literature can be well developed, creating round characters, or developed in a shallow way relying on generalizations, creating stereotype characters. A stereotype is an over generalized belief about a particular group or class of people. An example of a stereotype is that all kids who play sports get low grades or that all students who get high grades are socially awkward. Round characters often have aspects of their personalities which are unexpected in some way. For example, a teacher in a work of fiction who is a "round character" might also be an Olympic athlete. Stereotyped characters conform to generalized expectations. A teacher in a work of fiction who is stereotyped might be mean, unforgiving and strict.

From the list of characters below, put the names of round characters in the relevant boxes and names of stereotype characters in the relevant boxes. Complete the chart, using actual quotes when asked and noting page numbers. Go back and skim the text if you need to, to refresh your memory about these characters.

Lennie | George | Curley's wife | Slim | Candy | Carlson

Name of Round Character	Quote – Observation 1 (Find a quote that shows how a character has some unexpected quality.)	Quote – Observation 2 (Find a quote that shows how a character has some unexpected quality.)	How do the unexpected qualities shape your understanding of the character?

Name of Stereotype Character	Quote – Observation 1 (Find a quote that shows how a character has a quality that conforms to a stereotype.)	Quote – Observation 2 (Find a quote that shows how a character has a quality that conforms to a stereotype.)	Does the character conform to a stereotype? Describe the stereotype.

Of Mice and Men Chapter 5: Action, Character, Decision

Write **A** (for Action) **C** (for Character) or **D** (for Decision) in the blank next to each to identify whether the passage/statement advances the action, tells us more about a character, or provokes a decision. On the lines under each question, provide a short explanation of your choice.

____ 1. Suddenly his anger arose. "God damn you," he cried. "Why do you got to get killed? You ain't so little as mice." He picked up the pup and hurled it from him. He turned his back on it. He sat bent over his knees and he whispered, "Now I won't get to tend the rabbits. Now he won't let me." He rocked himself back and forth in his sorrow.

____ 2. Lennie said, "Well, I ain't supposed to talk to you or nothing."

____ 3. "I like to pet nice things. Once at a fair I seen some of them long-hair rabbits. An' they was nice, you bet. Sometimes I've even pet mice, but not when I couldn't get nothing better."

____ 4. "Feel right aroun' there an' see how soft it is." Lennie's big fingers fell to stroking her hair.

____ 5. "That big son-of-a-bitch done it. I know he done it. Why- ever'body else was out there playin' horseshoes." He worked himself into a fury. "I'm gonna get him. I'm going for my shotgun. I'll kill the big son-of-a-bitch myself. I'll shoot 'im in the guts. Come on, you guys." He ran furiously out of the barn. Carlson said, "I'll get my Luger," and he ran out too.

Of Mice And Men Chapter 5: Figurative Language

Read the following passages, and determine if the language is literal (L), simile (S), metaphor (M), onomatopoeia (O) or hyperbole (H). On the lines below, explain any use of figurative language and the effect it has on meaning.

____1. The hay came down like a mountain slope to the other end of the barn, and there was a level place as yet unfilled with the new crop.

____2. "Why can't I talk to you? I never get to talk to nobody. I get awful lonely."

____3. There was the buzz of flies in the air, the lazy afternoon humming.

____4. From outside came the clang of horseshoes on the iron stake, and then a little chorus of cries.

____5. His hair is jus' like wire.

Of Mice And Men Chapter 5: Elements of Fiction & Literary Devices

One of the primary themes in the novel is fear. Consider the following passages and how Steinbeck presents and defines the concept of fear.

1. Suddenly his anger arose. "God damn you," he cried. "Why do you got to get killed? You ain't so little as mice." He picked up the pup and hurled it from him.

Have similar situations been foreshadowed?

2. Curley's wife came around the end of the last stall. She came very quietly, so that Lennie didn't see her. She wore her bright cotton dress and the mules with the red ostrich feathers. Her face was made up and the little sausage curls were all in place. She was quite near to him before Lennie looked up and saw her.

Curley's wife is a character archetype patterned after the Biblical figure Eve from the story of The Garden of Eden. How does this description of her fit that archetype?

3. Her face grew angry. "Wha's the matter with me?" she cried. "Ain't I got a right to talk to nobody? Whatta they think I am, anyways? You're a nice guy. I don't know why I can't talk to you. I ain't doin' no harm to you."

This passage is very much about prejudice. Why is it ironic?

Of Mice And Men Chapter 5: Elements of Fiction & Literary Devices Page 2

4. Curley's wife lay with a half-covering of yellow hay. And the meanness and the plannings and the discontent and the ache for attention were all gone from her face. She was very pretty and simple, and her face was sweet and young. Now her rouged cheeks and her reddened lips made her seem alive and sleeping very lightly. The curls, tiny little sausages, were spread on the hay behind her head, and her lips were parted.

What does this description suggest about how women are presented in the novel?

5. As happens sometimes, a moment settled and hovered and remained for much more than a moment. And sound stopped and movement stopped for much, much more than a moment.

How does the passage connect to the theme of nature and cycles?

6. Old Candy watched him go. He looked helplessly back at Curley's wife, and gradually his sorrow and his anger grew into words. "You God damn tramp", he said viciously. "You done it, di'n't you? I s'pose you're glad. Ever'body knowed you'd mess things up. You wasn't no good. You ain't no good now, you lousy tart." He sniveled, and his voice shook. "I could of hoed in the garden and washed dishes for them guys." He paused, and then went on in a singsong. And he repeated the old words: "If they was a circus or a baseball game... we would of went to her... jus' said 'ta hell with work,' an' went to her. Never ast nobody's say so. An' they'd of been a pig and chickens... an' in the winter... the little fat stove... an' the rain comin'... an' us jes' settin' there." His eyes blinded with tears and he turned andwent weakly out of the barn, and he rubbed his bristly whiskers with his wrist stump.

How does this passage relate to the theme of freedom?

Of Mice And Men Chapter 5: Meaning & Inferences 1

Read the passages and answer the related questions.

1. *She moved closer to him and she spoke soothingly. "Don't you worry about talkin' to me. Listen to the guys yell out there. They got four dollars bet in that tenement. None of them ain't gonna leave till it's over."*

What is the connotation of the word "soothingly"?

2. *"Seems like they ain't none of them cares how I gotta live."*

What is the tone of the passage?

3. *Curley's wife said angrily, "Don't you think of nothing but rabbits?"*

Why does she say it "angrily"?

4. *He moved his hand a little and her hoarse cry came out. Then Lennie grew angry. "Now don't," he said. "I don't want you to yell. You gonna get me in trouble jus' like George says you will. Now don't you do that." And she continued to struggle, and her eyes were wild with terror. He shook her then, and he was angry with her. "Don't you go yellin'," he said, and he shook her; and her body flopped like a fish. And then she was still, for Lennie had broken her neck.*

Compare this passage to the description of Curley's fight with Lennie. What do they share in common? Why is this significant?

5. *Around the last stall came a shepherd bitch, lean and long, with heavy, hanging dugs. Halfway to the packing box where the puppies were she caught the dead scent of Curley's wife, and the hair arose along her spine. She whimpered and cringed to the packing box, and jumped in among the puppies.*

What does the dog's reaction suggest?

Of Mice and Men Chapter 5: Meaning & Inferences 2

Read the passage and answer the related questions.

She went on with her story quickly, before she should be interrupted. "'Nother time I met a guy, an' he was in pitchers. Went out to the Riverside Dance Palace with him. He says he was gonna put me in the movies. Says I was a natural. Soon's he got back to Hollywood he was gonna write to me about it." She looked closely at Lennie to see whether she was impressing him. "I never got that letter," she said. "I always thought my ol' lady stole it. Well, I wasn't gonna stay no place where I couldn't get nowhere or make something of myself, an' where they stole your letters. I ast her if she stole it, too, an' she says no. So I married Curley. Met him out to the Riverside Dance Palace that same night." She demanded, "You listenin'?"

"Me? Sure."

"Well, I ain't told this to nobody before. Maybe I oughten to. I don' like Curley. He ain't a nice fella." And because she had confided in him, she moved closer to Lennie and sat beside him. "Coulda been in the movies, an' had nice clothes- all them nice clothes like they wear. An' I coulda sat in them big hotels, an' had pitchers took of me. When they had them previews I coulda went to them, an' spoke in the radio, an' it wouldn'ta cost me a cent because I was in the pitcher. An' all them nice clothes like they wear. Because this guy says I was a natural." She looked up at Lennie, and she made a small grand gesture with her arm and hand to show that she could act. The fingers trailed after her leading wrist, and her little finger stuck out grandly from the rest.

1. How likely were Curley's wife's dreams to happen? Does she believe that they were likely to happen?

2. Why does she care if she is "impressing" Lennie?

3. Why does she marry Curley?

4. Compare the details of the Curley wife's dream to the farm.

Of Mice And Men Chapter 5: "What Does Curley's Wife Symbolize?"

Chapter 5 provides more insight into the only female character who is active and present within the novel. While other women are alluded to—Aunt Clara, the girl in Weed, and madams and prostitutes—only Curley's wife interacts with the novel's protagonists. As seen in Chapter 4, Curley's wife is an isolated character, and the depths of her desperation are explored more fully in Chapter 5 as she converses with Lennie.

Using textual evidence from Chapter 5, look for important but perhaps seemingly insignificant details to answer to the question: What does Curley's wife symbolize?

To define what Curley's wife symbolizes:

1. Identify passages and quotes which offer details about or insights into Curley's wife and her opinions about her past, present and future.

2. Examine the context of your quotes.

3. Consider the connotation and denotation of key phrases in your quotes.

4. Consider these points:
    a. Why does she feel so isolated?
    b. How does she feel about marriage? About Curley?
    c. What dreams does she believe in?
    d. Why is she so angry?
    e. Does she have empathy for Lennie? Did this contribute to the accident?
    f. Does she manipulate Lennie? Did this contribute to the accident?
    g. What do you think Steinbeck would say Curley's wife's role is in the story?
    h. What part of life or society do we see in Curley's wife?

Of Mice And Men Chapter 5: "What Does Curley's Wife Symbolize?" Page 2

Use Your Own Knowledge

1. What were cultural attitudes towards women in the 1930s?

2. What were the cultural expectations for married women in the 1930s?

3. Is Curley's wife a victim of the times she lived in?

Of Mice And Men Chapter 5: "What Does Curley's Wife Symbolize?" Page 3

Complete as many of these charts as you need to explore the symbolism of Curley's wife.

Find a quote about:	Quote (and page number)	Paraphrase Quote	How is isolation affecting the speaker?
Physical description of Curley's wife			
Curley's wife persuading Lennie to talk to her			
Curley's wife's "confessions" to Lennie about her past and her feelings about her marriage			
Others' attitudes or opinions about Curley's wife			

Of Mice and Men Chapter 5: Creative Analytical Writing Assignments

1. Write a flashback scene about Curley's wife's childhood.

2. Write a scene in dialogue of a conversation between Curley's wife and her mother about the probabilities of her dream coming true.

3. Write a scene that depicts Curley and his wife's first meeting.

4. Which dream seems more likely: becoming a movie star or buying a farm?

5. Why does Curley's wife "confess" to Lennie? Was Crooks right about Lennie's being perfect to talk to because he was not capable of retaining information?

6. Why do you think Lennie likes soft things?

7. How startled was Curley's wife by the sight of the dead puppy?

8. Imagine how Candy felt when he realized that buying a farm was unlikely, or more probably, impossible. Write a stream-of-consciousness paragraph about it.

9. Imagine how Curley felt when he realized that Lennie was probably responsible. Write a stream-of-consciousness paragraph about it.

10. Write a paragraph from George's perspective about why Lennie's killing someone was inevitable.

Of Mice and Men Chapter 5: Quick-Write Writing Assignments

1. Why does Curley's wife move so quietly?

2. What motivates Curley's wife to allow Lennie to touch her hair?

3. Is Lennie capable of running away and providing for himself?

4. Why does it matter that the men believe that Lennie stole Carlson's gun?

5. What does Carlson say about shooting Lennie? How does that relate to Candy's dog?

6. Besides George, who else understands exactly what is happening?

7. Is the death of Curley's wife sad?

8. Does Curley seem concerned about his wife's death? Does he seem to have grief about it?

9. How is Curley's wife objectified in the chapter?

10. Is Lennie dangerous? If so, why?

MATERIALS: CHAPTER 6
OF MICE AND MEN

Reading Activity 1: True or False?

Reading Activity 2: Analyzing Passages

Reading Activity 3: A Closer Look At Lennie

Reading Activity 4: Action, Character, Decision

Reading Activity 5: Figurative Language

Reading Activity 6: Elements of Fiction & Literary Devices

Reading Activity 7: Meaning and Inferences

Writing Activity 1: Is Murder An Act Of Friendship?

Suggested Writing Assignments

Quick-Write Assignments

NOTES
OF MICE AND MEN

Of Mice And Men Chapter 6: True or False?

Write *True* or *False* in the blank next to each statement. Below the statement, explain why you chose true or false, referencing the text to support your choices.

_____ 1. Aunt Clara is angry at Lennie.

_____ 2. Lennie's greatest fear seems to be George's leaving him.

_____ 3. Lennie begs George to yell at him.

Of Mice And Men Chapter 6: True or False? Page 2

_____ 4. George is very angry at Lennie.

_____ 5. George kills Lennie out of self-defense.

_____ 6. Slim is understanding and offers George support.

Of Mice And Men Chapter 6 True or False? Evaluation

List Your Group's Members: Your Group's Question # _____

_____   _____   _____

_____   _____   _____

1 = No, Not At All **2** = A Little **3** = Some **4** = Yes **5** = Yes, Very Well

Evaluation of Question # ___
Does the explanation support the answer of true or false?   1 2 3 4 5
Is there good textual evidence to support the answer?   1 2 3 4 5
Is the answer clearly stated?   1 2 3 4 5
                      Total Score _____ of a possible 15 points

Evaluation of Question # ___
Does the explanation support the answer of true or false?   1 2 3 4 5
Is there good textual evidence to support the answer?   1 2 3 4 5
Is the answer clearly stated?   1 2 3 4 5
                      Total Score _____ of a possible 15 points

Evaluation of Question # ___
Does the explanation support the answer of true or false?   1 2 3 4 5
Is there good textual evidence to support the answer?   1 2 3 4 5
Is the answer clearly stated?   1 2 3 4 5
                      Total Score _____ of a possible 15 points

Evaluation of Question # ___
Does the explanation support the answer of true or false?   1 2 3 4 5
Is there good textual evidence to support the answer?   1 2 3 4 5
Is the answer clearly stated?   1 2 3 4 5
                      Total Score _____ of a possible 15 points

Evaluation of Question # ___
Does the explanation support the answer of true or false?   1 2 3 4 5
Is there good textual evidence to support the answer?   1 2 3 4 5
Is the answer clearly stated?   1 2 3 4 5
                      Total Score _____ of a possible 15 points

Of Mice And Men Chapter 6 Analyzing Passages

Answer the questions following the quotations completely.

1. She stood in front of Lennie and put her hands on her hips, and she frowned disapprovingly at him.

 And when she spoke, it was in Lennie's voice. "I tol' you an tol' you," she said. "I tol you, 'Min' George because he's such a nice fella an' good to you.' But you don't never take no care. You do bad things."

Why does it matter that it is in Lennie's voice?

2. Lennie said, "George."
"Yeah?"
"I done another bad thing."
"It don't make no difference," George said, and he fell silent again.

What is George's tone?

3. Slim came directly to George and sat down beside him, sat very close to him. "Never you mind," said Slim. "A guy got to sometimes."

To what is Slim referring?

4. " Lennie said, "I thought you was mad at me, George."
"No," said George. "No, Lennie, I ain't mad. I never been mad, and I ain' now. That's a thing I want ya to know."

What does George's response imply?

5. "The deep green pool of the Salinas River was still in the late afternoon. Already the sun had left the valley to go climbing up the slopes of the Gabilan Mountains, and the hilltops were rosy in the sun. But by the pool among the mottled sycamores, a pleasant shade had fallen."

What is the significance of the light and dark imagery?

6. " Lennie begged, "Le's do it now. Le's get that place now."
"Sure, right now. I gotta. We gotta."
And George raised the gun and steadied it, and he brought the muzzle of it close to the back of Lennie's head. The hand shook violently, but his face set and his hand steadied. He pulled the trigger. The crash of the shot rolled up the hills and rolled down again. Lennie jarred, and then settled slowly forward to the sand, and he lay without quivering."

How does this passage show George's conflict?

Of Mice And Men Chapter 6 Analyzing Passages Page 3

7. But George sat stiffly on the bank and looked at his right hand that had thrown the gun away. The group burst into the clearing, and Curley was ahead. He saw Lennie lying on the sand. "Got him, by God." He went over and looked down at Lennie, and then he looked back at George. "Right in the back of the head," he said softly.

What is Curley's response? Why is it ironic?

8. Curley and Carlson looked after them. And Carlson said, "Now what the hell ya suppose is eatin' them two guys?"

How are George and Slim atypical?

Of Mice And Men Chapter 6 Reading Activity 3: A Closer Look at Lennie

The majority of the novel offers a third person perspective of Lennie. The narrator conveys what Lennie feels but in a way that is moderated.

Chapter 6 is unusual in that it gives insights into Lennie that are radically different from the previous chapters. Lennie's hallucinations of his Aunt Clara and of a giant rabbit are presented as Lennie himself perceives them. This additional information provides characterization for fully understanding Lennie.

Quote	What does this suggest about Lennie?	How does this portray Lennie in a different way?	Does it make Lennie more or less sympathetic?
Quote that Aunt Clara says			
Quote that Lennie says to Aunt Clara			
Quote that giant rabbit says			
Quote that Lennie says to giant rabbit			

Of Mice And Men Chapter 6: Action, Character, Decision

Write **A** (for Action) **C** (for Character) or **D** (for Decision) in the blank next to each to identify whether the passage/statement advances the action, tells us more about a character, or provokes a decision. On the lines under each question, provide a short explanation of your choice.

___ 1. Aunt Clara was gone, and from out of Lennie's head there came a gigantic rabbit.

___ 2. George shook himself again. "No," he said. "I want you to stay with me here."

___ 3. "Go on," said Lennie. "How's it gonna be. We gonna get a little place."

___ 4. "No, Lennie. I ain't mad. I never been mad, an' I ain't now. That's a thing I want ya to know."

___ 5. Slim came directly to George and sat down beside him, sat very close to him.

Of Mice And Men Chapter 6: Figurative Language

Read the following passages, and determine if the language is literal (L), simile (S), metaphor (M), personification (P) or hyperbole (H). On the lines below, explain any use of figurative language and the effect it has on meaning.

_____1. A far rush of wind sounded and a gust drove through the tops of the trees like a wave.

_____2. Another little water snake swam up the pool, turning its periscope head from side to side.

_____3. It sat on its haunches in front of him, and it waggled its ears and crinkled its nose at him. And it spoke in Lennie's voice too.

_____4. "You ain't worth a greased jack-pin to ram you into hell.

_____5. George let himself be helped to his feet.

Of Mice And Men Chapter 6: Elements of Fiction & Literary Devices

One of the elements of fiction is setting, or the time and place in which action occurs. Consider the quotes below and answer questions about the significance of the setting.

1. The deep green pool of the Salinas River was still in the late afternoon. Already the sun had left the valley to go climbing up the slopes of the Gabilan Mountains, and the hilltops were rosy in the sun. But by the pool among the mottled sycamores, a pleasant shade had fallen.

What does the relationship of sun and shade to the hiding place suggest about the novel's denouement?

_____
_____
_____
_____
_____

2. A water snake glided smoothly up the pool, twisting its periscope head from side to side; and it swam the length of the pool and came to the legs of a motionless heron that stood in the shallows. A silent head and beak lanced down and plucked it out by the head, and the beak swallowed the little snake while its tail waved frantically.

What is the significance of this detail? What themes does it relate to?

_____
_____
_____
_____
_____

3. Suddenly Lennie appeared out of the brush, and he came as silently as a creeping bear moves. The heron pounded the air with its wings, jacked itself clear of the water and flew off down river. The little snake slid in among the reeds at the pool's side.

What is Lennie's relationship to the landscape, according to the text?

_____
_____
_____
_____
_____

4. Only the topmost ridges were in the sun now. The shadow in the valley was blue and soft. From the distance came the sound of men shouting to one another. George turned his head and listened to the shouts.

The shifting of the light parallels what action occurring in the text?

5. Lennie removed his hat dutifully and laid it on the ground in front of him. The shadow in the valley was bluer, and the evening came fast. On the wind the sound of crashing in the brush came to them.

What does the wind signify here? What "message" does it deliver?

6. And George raised the gun and steadied it, and he brought the muzzle of it close to the back of Lennie's head. The hand shook violently, but his face set and his hand steadied. He pulled the trigger. The crash of the shot rolled up the hills and rolled down again. Lennie jarred, and then settled slowly forward to the sand, and he lay without quivering.

How and why does a mention of the landscape interrupt the narration of Lennie's death?

Of Mice And Men Chapter 6: Meaning & Inferences 1

Read the passages and answer the related questions.

1. *And then from out of Lennie's head there came a little fat old woman. She wore thick bull's-eye glasses and she wore a huge gingham apron with pockets, and she was starched and clean. She stood in front of Lennie and put her hands on her hips, and she frowned disapprovingly at him.*

What was Aunt Clara probably like in real life?

2. *"Tend rabbits," it said scornfully. "You crazy bastard. You ain't fit to lick the boots of no rabbit. You'd forget 'em and let 'em go hungry. That's what you'd do. An' then what would George think?"*

How does the rabbit offend Lennie? What is the ultimate offense?

3. *But the rabbit repeated softly over and over, "He gonna leave you, ya crazy bastard. He gonna leave ya all alone. He gonna leave ya crazy bastard."*

What is the effect of the repetition?

4. *"Sure, like you always done before. Like, 'If I di'n't have you I'd take my fifty bucks-'"*

Why is it significant that Lennie quotes George?

Of Mice And Men Chapter 6: Meaning & Inferences 1 Page 2

5. *"No, Lennie. Look down there acrost the river, like you can almost see the place."*
Lennie obeyed him. George looked down at the gun. There were crashing footsteps in the brush now. George turned and looked toward them.
"Go on, George. When we gonna do it?"
"Gonna do it soon."
"Me an' you."
"You... an' me. Ever'body gonna be nice to you. Ain't gonna be no more trouble. Nobody gonna hurt nobody nor steal from 'em."

Does Lennie achieve the dream?

Of Mice And Men Chapter 6: Meaning & Inferences 2

Read the passage and answer the related questions.

George came quietly out of the brush and the rabbit scuttled back into Lennie's brain.
George said quietly, "What the hell you yellin' about?"
Lennie got up on his knees. "You ain't gonna leave me, are ya, George? I know you ain't."
George came stiffly near and sat down beside him. "No."
"I knowed it," Lennie cried. "You ain't that kind."
George was silent.
Lennie said, "George."
"Yeah?"
"I done another bad thing."
"It don't make no difference," George said, and he fell silent again.
Only the topmost ridges were in the sun now. The shadow in the valley was blue and soft. From the distance came the sound of men shouting to one another. George turned his head and listened to the shouts.
Lennie said, "George."
"Yeah?"
"Ain't you gonna give me hell?"
"Give ya hell?"
"Sure, like you always done before. Like, 'If I di'n't have you I'd take my fifty bucks-'"
"Jesus Christ, Lennie! You can't remember nothing that happens, but you remember ever' word I say."
"Well, ain't you gonna say it?"
George shook himself. He said woodenly, "If I was alone I could live so easy." His voice was monotonous, had no emphasis. "I could get a job an' not have no mess." He stopped.
"Go on," said Lennie. "An' when the enda the month come-"
"An' when the end of the month came I could take my fifty bucks an' go to a... cat house..." He stopped again.
Lennie looked eagerly at him. "Go on, George. Ain't you gonna give me no more hell?"
"No," said George.
"Well, I can go away," said Lennie. "I'll go right off in the hills an' find a cave if you don' want me."
George shook himself again. "No," he said. "I want you to stay with me here."

1. If George's presence makes the rabbit disappear, what does that suggest about the rabbit? About Lennie's relationship with George?

2. Compare this passage to the opening scene of the novel. Why is George's silence here noteworthy?

3. Why does Lennie want George to yell at him?

4. What is the tone of George's reproach? If he doesn't want to yell at Lennie, why does he do it?

Of Mice And Men Chapter 6: "Is Murder An Act Of Friendship?"

Write a paper in which you analyze the following statement and take a position in agreement with or in opposition to it:

George kills Lennie in the final scene of the novel as an act of friendship.

To evaluate the statement:

1. Identify passages and quotes which offer details about or insights into Steinbeck's notions of friendship.
   - How do Lennie and George define their friendship
   - Lennie and George
     - The boss's and Curley's reaction to their friendship
     - Slim's reaction to their friendship

2. Examine the context of your quotes.

3. Consider the connotation and denotation of key phrases in your quotes.

   a. What does George gain through his friendship with Lennie?
   b. What does Lennie gain through his friendship with George?
   c. What makes the friendship challenging for George?
   d. What makes the friendship challenging for Lennie?
   e. What alternatives does George have?

Of Mice And Men Chapter 6: "Is Murder An Act Of Friendship?" Page 2

Use Your Own Knowledge

1. How do you think most people define friendship?

2. What responsibility does one friend have for another?

3. What is Lennie's greatest fear? How does George's decision relate to it?

Of Mice And Men Chapter 6: "Is Murder An Act Of Friendship?" Page 3

Complete as many of these charts as you need to explore the concept of friendship. In the final scene between George and Lennie, George says and does things but intends a different meaning. Find moments from the text when these double or unintended meanings occur.

Quote (and page number)	Paraphrase Quote	What is its intended meaning?	What is its double/unintended meaning? (What is George actually saying/conveying?)
Example: George took off his hat. He said shakily, "Take off your hat, Lennie. The air feels fine."	Lennie, take off your hat.	That Lennie would enjoy feeling the evening air.	He is preparing to shoot Lennie and finds a gentle and misleading way to get Lennie ready.

Of Mice And Men Chapter 6: Creative Analytical Writing Assignments

1. Write a scene of dialogue between Lennie and "Aunt Clara" at a different point in the novel.

2. Write a scene of dialogue between Lennie and "the gigantic rabbit" at a different point in the novel.

3. Write a stream of consciousness paragraph about the thought racing through George's mind as he shoots Lennie.

4. Write a eulogy for Lennie from George's perspective.

5. Write an epilogue that explains if George ever believed in the dream again.

6. Study the Robert Burns poem from which the novel borrows its title. Write a poem inspired by the novel.

7. Write the final scene from a different character's perspective (Slim, Carlson or Curley).

8. Write the final scene from the perspective of the landscape. What do the heron, snake and birds see?

9. Write a newspaper article about Lennie's death.

10. Describe how Lennie was like a bear. What animal is George like?

Of Mice And Men Chapter 6: Quick-Write Writing Assignments

1. Why did George kill Lennie?
2. Why does Lennie beg George to yell at him?
3. What is George's tone toward Lennie?
4. Is Lennie "nuts," as Crooks suggested earlier in the novel?
5. Does Lennie achieve the dream?
6. What is the most suspenseful moment of the novel?
7. Compare Slim and Carlson.
8. Does George's act of killing provide justice?
9. Do any of the characters actually understand friendship?
10. Why is it significant that the novel ends in the place where it began?

NOTES
OF MICE AND MEN

MATERIALS: OVERVIEW
OF MICE AND MEN

Reading Activity 1: True or False?

Reading Activity 2: Analyzing Passages

Reading Activity 3: Characters, Motivation, and Dreams

Reading Activity 4: Action, Character, Decision

Reading Activity 5: Figurative Language

Reading Activity 6: Elements of Fiction & Literary Devices

Reading Activity 7: Meaning and Inferences

Writing Activity 1: Is Sharing A Common Dream Possible?

Suggested Writing Assignments

Quick-Write Assignments

NOTES
OF MICE AND MEN

Of Mice And Men Overview: True or False?

Write *True* or *False* in the blank next to each statement. Below the statement, explain why you chose true or false, referencing the text to support your choices.

_____ 1. Lennie stole Carlson's gun.

_____ 2. Candy lost his hand in a farming accident.

_____ 3. George almost caused Lennie to drown.

Of Mice And Men Overview True or False? Page 2

_____ 4. Candy is threatened with being lynched.

_____ 5. George admits to himself that he always knew the dream was unattainable.

_____ 6. Slim believes that George's killing of Lennie is irresponsible.

Of Mice And Men Overview True or False? Evaluation

List Your Group's Members: Your Group's Question # _____

_____   _____   _____

_____   _____   _____

1 = No, Not At All 2 = A Little 3 = Some 4 = Yes 5 = Yes, Very Well

Evaluation of Question # ___
Does the explanation support the answer of true or false?   1 2 3 4 5
Is there good textual evidence to support the answer?   1 2 3 4 5
Is the answer clearly stated?   1 2 3 4 5
                        Total Score _____ of a possible 15 points

Evaluation of Question # ___
Does the explanation support the answer of true or false?   1 2 3 4 5
Is there good textual evidence to support the answer?   1 2 3 4 5
Is the answer clearly stated?   1 2 3 4 5
                        Total Score _____ of a possible 15 points

Evaluation of Question # ___
Does the explanation support the answer of true or false?   1 2 3 4 5
Is there good textual evidence to support the answer?   1 2 3 4 5
Is the answer clearly stated?   1 2 3 4 5
                        Total Score _____ of a possible 15 points

Evaluation of Question # ___
Does the explanation support the answer of true or false?   1 2 3 4 5
Is there good textual evidence to support the answer?   1 2 3 4 5
Is the answer clearly stated?   1 2 3 4 5
                        Total Score _____ of a possible 15 points

Evaluation of Question # ___
Does the explanation support the answer of true or false?   1 2 3 4 5
Is there good textual evidence to support the answer?   1 2 3 4 5
Is the answer clearly stated?   1 2 3 4 5
                        Total Score _____ of a possible 15 points

Of Mice And Men Overview Analyzing Passages

Answer the questions following the quotations completely.

1. Evening of a hot day started the little wind to moving among the leaves. The shade climbed up the hills toward the top. On the sand banks the rabbits sat as quietly as little gray sculptured stones. And then from the direction of the state highway came the sound of footsteps on crisp sycamore leaves. The rabbits hurried noiselessly for cover. A stilted heron labored up into the air and pounded down river. For a moment the place was lifeless, and then two men emerged from the path and came into the opening by the green pool.

What do rabbits symbolize?

_____
_____
_____

2. A guy sets alone out here at night, maybe readin' books or thinkin' or stuff like that. Sometimes he gets thinkin', an' he got nothing to tell him what's so an' what ain't so. Maybe if he sees somethin', he don't know whether it's right or not. He can't turn to some other guy and ast him if he sees it too. He can't tell. He got nothing to measure by. I seen things out here. I wasn't drunk. I don't know if I was asleep. If some guy was with me, he could tell me I was asleep, an' then it would be all right. But I jus' don't know.

What does "measure" mean here?

_____
_____
_____

3. George looked around at Lennie. "Jesus, what a tramp," he said. "So that's what Curley picks for a wife." "She's purty," said Lennie defensively. "Yeah, and she's sure hidin' it. Curley got his work ahead of him. Bet she'd clear out for twenty bucks."

Lennie still stared at the doorway where she had been. "Gosh, she was purty." He smiled admiringly.

George looked quickly down at him and then he took him by an ear and shook him. "Listen to me, you crazy bastard," he said fiercely. "Don't you even take a look at that bitch. I don't care what she says and what she does. I seen 'em poison before, but I never seen no piece of jail bait worse than her. You leave her be."

Why is it significant that Curley's wife is never given a name, but referred to by different terms?

_____
_____
_____

Of Mice And Men Overview Analyzing Passages Page 2

4. Crooks reached around and explored his spine with his hand. "I never seen a guy really do it," he said. "I seen guys nearly crazy with loneliness for land, but ever' time a whore house or a blackjack game took what it takes." He hesitated. " . . . . If you . . . . guys would want a hand to work for nothing—just his keep, why I'd come an' lend a hand. I ain't so crippled I can't work like a son-of-a- bitch if I want to."

How are Candy and Crooks similar?

_____
_____
_____

5. Slim twitched George's elbow. "Come on, George. Me an' you'll go in an' get a drink." George let himself be helped to his feet. "Yeah, a drink." Slim said, "You hadda, George. I swear you hadda. Come on with me." He led George into the entrance of the trail and up toward the highway.

How do Slim's actions show his personality?

_____
_____
_____

6. Curley's wife lay with a half-covering of yellow hay. And the meanness and the plannings and the discontent and the ache for attention were all gone from her face. She was very pretty and simple, and her face was sweet and young. Now her rouged cheeks and her reddened lips made her seem alive and sleeping very lightly. The curls, tiny little sausages, were spread on the hay behind her head, and her lips were parted.

In what ways is Curley's wife different in death than in life?

_____
_____
_____

7. "A water snake glided smoothly up the pool, twisting its periscope head from side to side; and it swam the length of the pool and came to the legs of a motionless heron that stood in the shallows. A silent head and beak lanced down and plucked it out by the head, and the beak swallowed the little snake while its tail waved frantically."

What is the significance of the natural world in the novel?

_____
_____
_____

Of Mice And Men Overview
Reading Activity 3: Characters, Motivation, and Dreams

Select one of the characters from the list below. Imagine that character at an earlier time in the character's life, sometime before the action of the novel begins.

Candy   Curley   Slim   Carlson   Curley's Wife   Crooks

Step 1: Answer this question: What is this character's main personal dream? To answer the question, think about the character's actions and interests. How could these have fit the goals and ambitions of the character at another point in his or her life?

_____
_____
_____
_____
_____

Step 2: Find a relevant passage in the novel and copy it below. Think about the dream you identified for the character you selected. Is there a point in the novel where we could imagine a flashback when this character's dream is somehow and for some reason revealed?

_____
_____
_____
_____
_____
_____
_____
_____
_____

Of Mice And Men Overview Reading Activity 3: Characters, Motivation, and Dreams Page 2

Step 3: Writing the flashback: On the lines below, write a flashback that is 3 paragraphs long that shows how and why your character believes in their dream. Be descriptive, use dialogue and use details from the novel.

Of Mice And Men Overview: Action, Character, Decision

Write **A** (for Action) **C** (for Character) or **D** (for Decision) in the blank next to each to identify whether the passage/statement advances the action, tells us more about a character, or provokes a decision. On the lines under each question, provide a short explanation of your choice.

____ 1. "'Course you did. Well, look. Lennie- if you jus' happen to get in trouble like you always done before, I want you to come right here an' hide in the brush."

____ 2. His arms gradually bent at the elbows and his hands closed into fists. He stiffened and went into a slight crouch. His glance was at once calculating and pugnacious.

____ 3. "Listen to me, you crazy bastard," he said fiercely. "Don't you even take a look at that bitch. I don't care what she says and what she does. I seen 'em poison before, but I never seen no piece of jail bait worse than her. You leave her be."

____ 4. Crooks had reduced himself to nothing. There was no personality, no ego- nothing to arouse either like or dislike.

____ 5. She struggled violently under his hands. Her feet battered on the hay and she writhed to be free; and from under Lennie's hand came a muffled screaming. Lennie began to cry with fright.

Of Mice And Men Overview: Figurative Language

Read the following passages and determine if the passage contains hyperbole (H) or metaphor (M). On the lines below, explain how figurative language create meaning in the passage.

____1. Behind him walked his opposite, a huge man, shapeless of face, with large, pale eyes, and wide, sloping shoulders; and he walked heavily, dragging his feet a little, the way a bear drags his paws. His arms did not swing at his sides, but hung loosely.

____2. He was a jerkline skinner, the prince of the ranch, capable of driving ten, sixteen, even twenty mules with a single line to the leaders.

____3. 3. You jus' let 'em try to get the rabbits. I'll break their God damn necks. I'll . . . . I'll smash 'em with a stick." He subsided, grumbling to himself, threatening the future cats which might dare to disturb the future rabbits.

____4. Crooks bored in on him. "Want me ta tell ya what'll happen? They'll take ya to the booby hatch. They'll tie ya up with a collar, like a dog."

Of Mice And Men Overview: Elements of Fiction & Literary Devices

Explain how the following foreshadow future events in the novel.

1. Lennie's petting dead mice

2. The incident in Weed

3. George's escape plan

4. The death of Candy's dog.

5. Lennie's breaking Curley's hand

6. Lennie's being fascinated by Curley's wife

7. The death of Lennie's puppy

Of Mice And Men Overview: Meaning & Inferences 1

Read the passages and answer the related questions.

1. *George put his hand on Lennie's shoulder. "I ain't takin' it away jus' for meanness. That mouse ain't fresh, Lennie; and besides, you've broke it pettin' it. You get another mouse that's fresh and I'll let you keep it a little while."*

   What doesn't Lennie understand about keeping the mouse?

2. *Slim looked through George and beyond him. "Ain't many guys travel around together," he mused. "I don't know why. Maybe ever'body in the whole damn world is scared of each other."*

   What is Slim suggesting about "guys"? Why is "ever'body" significant?

3. *"You seen what they done to my dog tonight? They says he wasn't no good to himself nor nobody else. When they can me here I wisht somebody'd shoot me. But they won't do nothing like that. I won't have no place to go, an' I can't get no more jobs.*

   In what ways is Candy identifying with his dog?

Of Mice And Men Overview: Meaning & Inferences 1 Page 2

4. "'Member what I said about hoein' and doin' odd jobs?"
"Yeah," said Candy. "I remember."
"Well, jus' forget it," said Crooks. "I didn't mean it. Jus' foolin'. I wouldn' want to go no place like that."

How does Crooks's changing his mind relate to fear?

5. *He moved his hand a little and her hoarse cry came out. Then Lennie grew angry. "Now don't," he said. "I don't want you to yell. You gonna get me in trouble jus' like George says you will. Now don't you do that." And she continued to struggle, and her eyes were wild with terror. He shook her then, and he was angry with her. "Don't you go yellin'," he said, and he shook her; and her body flopped like a fish. And then she was still, for Lennie had broken her neck.*

Compare this passage to the description of Curley's fight with Lennie. What do they share in common? Why is this significant?

Of Mice And Men Overview: Meaning & Inferences 2

Read the passage and answer the related questions.

Guys like us, that work on ranches, are the loneliest guys in the world. They got no family. They don't belong no place. . . . With us it ain't like that. We got a future. We got somebody to talk to that gives a damn about us. We don't have to sit in no bar room blowin' in our jack jus' because we got no place else to go. If them other guys gets in jail they can rot for all anybody gives a damn. But not us.

1. What is the effect of the excessive use of pronouns in this passage?

2. Why, according to George, do most ranchers participate in counterproductive behaviors?

3. What is the cost of being isolated? What is the benefit of being together?

Of Mice And Men Overview: "Is Sharing A Common Dream Possible?"

One of the central themes in *Of Mice and Men* is that many of the characters are working to unite with one another. They share a collective dream and are working to realize that dream. However, there are forces at work that divide them and keep them from achieving this dream. Write a paper in which you (a) characterize their common dream and (b) explain at least two forces that keep this dream from becoming a reality.

To explore the idea of sharing a common dream:

1. Identify passages and quotes about the characters who have shared dreams.

2. Examine the context of your quotes.

3. Consider the connotation and denotation of key phrases in your quotes.
    a. What is the tone?
    b. Is there a conflict?
    c. What forces keep characters from uniting?
    d. Can those forces realistically be overcome?

4. Look for patterns in your evidence. Is a word or idea repeated? Use these patterns to shape an answer to the question.

Of Mice And Men Overview: "Is Sharing A Common Dream Possible?" Page 2

Complete the chart to analyze information to develop ideas to write your essay.

Describe the dream	Who believes in the dream?	What obstacles do they face in achieving their dream?	Can the obstacles be overcome? How or why not?

Of Mice And Men Overview: "Is Sharing A Common Dream Possible?" Page 3

Evaluate Your Textual Evidence

1. What societal beliefs hold the characters back from achieving their dreams?

2. How do the characters feel about these societal beliefs?

3. What motivates the characters?

Of Mice and Men Novel Overview: Creative Analytical Writing Assignments

1. Write the story of Candy's dog, recalling its vitality and youth.
2. What is George thinking as he shoots Lennie?
3. Will Lennie and Slim become friends?
4. Write a narrative description of Candy shooting the dog.
5. Does Curley believe that justice was served?
6. Write a description of the ranch from Curley's wife's perspective.
7. Define friendship.
8. Write a newspaper article about Lennie's death.
9. Write the final scene from a different character's perspective (Slim, Carlson or Curley).
10. Write a eulogy for Lennie from George's perspective.

Of Mice and Men Novel Overview: Quick-Write Writing Assignments

1. Is George responsible for Lennie?
2. Is Lennie "nuts"?
3. Is Curley's wife misunderstood?
4. Which character is most mistreated? Why?
5. Why is it significant that George mentions his "stake" so many times?
6. Why does Slim have so much moral authority?
7. Could Crooks be less isolated?
8. What roles does prejudice play in the novel?
9. How is farming a form of domestication? Are mice, puppies and rabbits domesticated?
10. Are the foreshadows too literal?

www.ingramcontent.com/pod-product-compliance
Lightning Source LLC
Chambersburg PA
CBHW081449070526
44586CB00019B/2280